MESOZOIC PARK
TERRY MUNRO

black dog press

CONTENTS

THE PALAEONTOLOGY OF THE PRESENT

—

TERRY MUNRO'S MESOZOIC PARK PHOTOGRAPHS

—

DANIELLE SIEMENS

"Photography is a tool for dealing with things everybody knows about but isn't attending to. My photographs are intended to represent something you don't see."
Emmet Gowin[1]

In Alberta, the Calgary Zoo is iconic. With over 120 acres of land on the banks of the Bow River, Canada's most visited zoo includes ambitious exhibits on the flora and fauna of Africa, Canada, and Eurasia as well as the Prehistoric Park within it, here renamed "Mesozoic Park", featuring life-sized dinosaur replicas in a constructed landscape. The latter includes facsimiles of mountains, hoodoos, and a volcano, in addition to over 100 species of living plants intended to simulate aspects of the Mesozoic Era and engage visitors in the fantasy of time travel. Designed to mimic a geological period that existed from 250 to 65 million years ago, this pseudo-prehistoric park has attracted local visitors and tourists alike for over 80 years, appealing to humanity's ever-increasing quest to find substitutes for the real.

Calgary-based photographer Terry Munro visited the site several times in 1982, simultaneously recording the rapidly changing landscape and the irony of the construction.[2] Today, his *Mesozoic Park* photographs offer privileged access to what we rarely get to see: the manufacturing of an artificial environment, of an attraction designed to provide visitors with a surrogate experience of nature and history. Best viewed in series, the images present a landscape of forgery, a facsimile that slowly unfolds through close scrutiny of the finely captured details.

What at first appears to be the site of an archaeological dig–industrial machinery, scaffolding, a drop cloth–gradually reveals itself as a construction site. The landscape, it seems, is not being excavated to reveal layers of geological history; rather, it is being fabricated from the ground up. Supported by dense scaffolding, mountains are built upon cinder blocks and rebar (fig. 3); the striations of hoodoos are achieved through deliberate placement of steel pipe (fig. 9); and metal mesh is molded into curvilinear forms (fig.8). A closer look still, and one notices seemingly innocuous details such as a street lamp extending beyond the summit of a craggy peak (fig. 18), electrical wiring running above a vista of hoodoos (fig. 6), and a multi-story tower on the horizon (fig. 10) that betray the urban setting and further suggest that this place is not all that it first appears to be.

Shot in black and white and with exacting detail, Munro's photographs document the fabrication of a geological dream world. The Prehistoric Park is an imaginative combination of climates and geologies representing an era that lasted 180 million years. It is an interpretation of the past using materials, both man-made and natural, that are readily available today. Designed and programmed for an artificial visitor experience, it is, to borrow a term from Jean Baudrillard, a "hyperreal" landscape, a model of the real "without origin or reality."[3] Baudrillard was among the first to moot the idea that in the postmodern age we are confronted with a *precession* of simulacra; that is, the representation precedes and determines the real. There is no longer any distinction between reality and its representation; there is only the simulacrum. It is the Park *as* simulacrum that Munro is concerned with interrogating and, by focusing his camera on that which we are not usually permitted to see, he brings awareness to a site that has been subjected to little public scrutiny.

Munro is, in the most general sense of the term, a landscape photographer, yet his interest lies not with the pristine, untouched wilderness but rather with what he terms "landscapes of capital." From Bedrock City in Kelowna to the Las Vegas Strip, Munro has focused his camera on the manufactured and commodified landscape–sites of architecture and nature packaged for human pleasure and consumption. His work as such can be situated within a paradigm

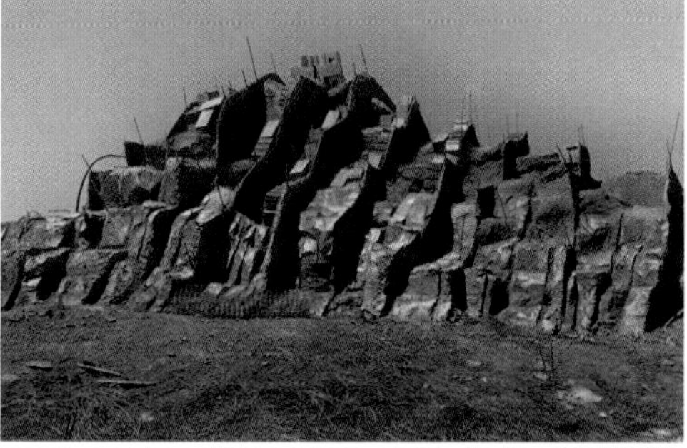

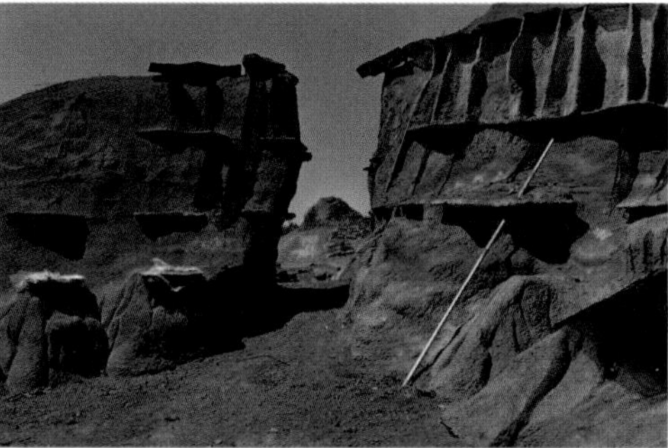

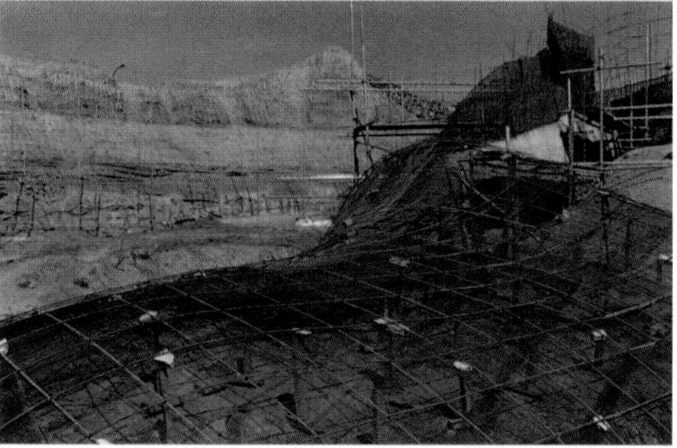

from top
Fig. 3; Fig. 9; Fig. 8

1
Emmett Gowin quoted in Susan Sontag, *On Photography* (New York: Farrar, Straus and Giroux, 1977), 200.

2
The Prehistoric Park first opened in 1937. In the early 1980s it was relocated, underwent a major renovation and was reopened in two phases in 1983 and 1984.

3
Jean Baudrillard, *Simulacra and Simulation*, trans. Sheila Faria Glaser (Paris: Éditions Galilée, 1981; Ann Arbor: The University of Michigan Press, 1994), 1. Citations refer to the reprint.

shift in contemporary landscape photography that began in the 1970s when photographers, many of whom were located in the American West, expanded the idea of scenic beauty to focus their cameras on the everyday.

Referred to now as New Topographic photographers, these image-makers posited an aesthetic of the banal, making photographs that framed suburban communities, industrial landscapes, and other quotidian subjects with matter-of-fact realism. Photographers including Robert Adams, Lewis Baltz, and Bernd and Hilla Becher have since inspired artists around the world "to make images that revealed landscapes as suitable places for social and political inquiry."[4] A younger generation of photographers, including Munro, are, in the words of art critic Dave Hickey, "informed by the suspicion that the way we represent the landscape is somehow complicit in our exploitation of it." These artists thus "aspire to portray nature differently," to portray a nature "that is as chaotic, dynamic, and historical as culture itself."[5] By photographing the Prehistoric Park in its stages of construction, Munro offers this banal and unsightly view as one deserving of our attention, asserting that it is equally, if not more, important than the final product. He reveals the artifice below the surface and asks of his viewers to consider what lengths humans are prepared to go to achieve a simulation of the real.[6]

Munro works within a deadpan aesthetic that lends itself well to his subject matter. Shooting in flat light and with a straightforward view, he focuses on registering the details of his environment in an effort to objectively reveal the realities of place. In the case of the *Mesozoic Park* images, these formal techniques also work to amplify the absurdity of place. In contemporary photography discourse the term "deadpan" has been used to describe an emotionally detached aesthetic that privileges visual information over beauty, emotion, or critique. While taking form in the early 1990s, the origins of this approach can be traced to the mid-1960s, particularly to the work of Ed Ruscha and the late Düsseldorf based artists Bernd and Hilla Becher. The only non-American photographers included in William Jenkins's groundbreaking exhibition *New Topographics: Photographs of a man-altered landscape* (1975), the Bechers are best known for their systematic documentation of industrial architectural structures such as water towers and coal breakers.[7] Striving to eliminate any trace of subjectivity in their photographs, the Bechers worked exclusively in black and white, shooting on overcast days and from a fixed vantage point. By displaying variant examples of a single type of building in grid formations, or what they called "typologies," the Bechers encouraged their viewers to examine both the intricacies of individual structures and the subtle differences between them.[8] In her theorizing on the deadpan in contemporary photography, Charlotte Cotton has suggested that deadpan "images seem to be products of an objective gaze in which the subject, rather than the photographer's perspective on it, is paramount."[9] She contends, moreover, that while a picture may engage with an emotive subject, the photographer's personal emotions or political views are not offered as a clear way of reading the image.[10] Munro's own critique is concealed behind the objective look of his images yet in the very act of picturing this landscape—in selecting and seeking out this site, returning to it over several visits, and attentively documenting its transformed topography—he presents the Prehistoric Park as a landscape of critical inquiry.[11] Moreover, his use of this aesthetic encourages viewers to look and to look again; to scrutinize the details of his images and ruminate on what it means to sculpt the earth into falsified form and to engage with a commodified landscape of imitation.

In 2018 Munro returned to the Prehistoric Park to re-photograph the site. Shot again in black and white, the images are stylistically linked to the earlier series yet the scenes they record are drastically transformed. Rebar and cinder blocks have been

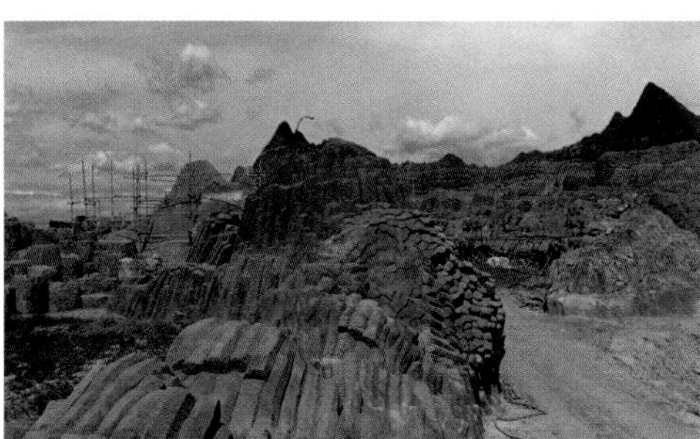

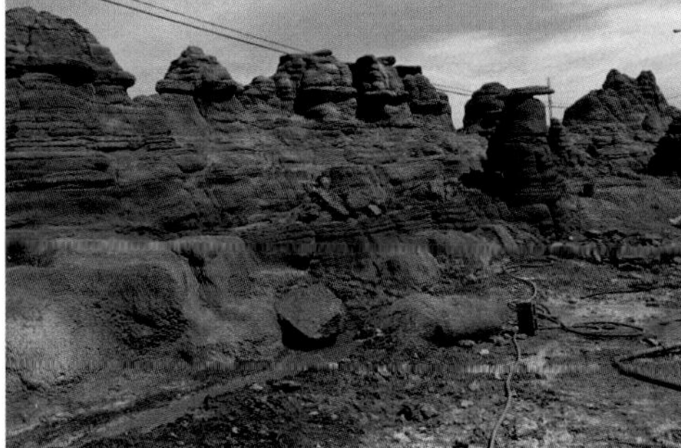

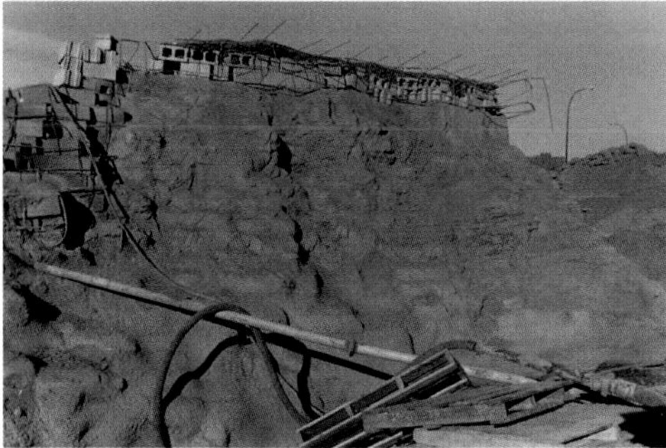

from top
Fig. 18; Fig. 6; Fig. 10

4
Ann M. Wolfe, "The Altered Landscape," in *The Altered Landscape: Photographs of a Changing Environment*, ed. Ann M. Wolfe (New York: Skira Rizzoli, 2011), 134. Exhibition catalogue, The Nevada Museum of Art, September 24, 2011 – January 8, 2012, 134.

5
Dave Hickey, "Shooting the Land," in *The Altered Landscape*, ed. Peter E. Pool (Reno/Las Vegas: Nevada Museum of Art in association with the University of Nevada Press, 1999), 25.

6
Munro is also influenced by the work of "land artists" such as Robert Smithson and Michael Heizer, who took their practice outside of the studio to utilize the land as their medium, either sculpting the earth itself or using natural materials to make new forms. While land artists operate in opposition to the commercial values that built the Prehistoric Park, Munro is interested in how they shape the earth into sculptural forms. Land art, moreover, is often ephemeral in nature and documented for posterity through photographs. Munro's photographs too are the lasting trace of the Park's construction and, like contemporary earthworks, they prod us to look anew at the world around us.

7
Their sharply focused, detached style founds its source in the German Neue Sachlichkeit (New Objectivity) movement that emerged in the 1920s with the work of photographers such as Karl Blossfeldt, Albert Renger-Patzsch, and August Sander, who rejected the sentimentality of Pictorialism.

8
This encyclopedic style and method of comparative display also references late nineteenth and early twentieth photographs of the natural sciences. By working within a formal approach that recalls the ways in which botany and zoology have historically been represented, Munro positions his images as objective views while also calling into question the verisimilitude of the photographic image.

9
Charlotte Cotton, *The Photograph as Contemporary Art*, 3rd ed. (London: Thames & Hudson, 2014), 9.

10
Ibid., 81. An interview with contemporary German photographer Kai-Olaf Hesse also offers an interesting analysis of the deadpan aesthetic. Hesse concludes that a "disimpassioned" presentation is not necessarily the result of a disimpassioned photographer; in fact, usually the opposite is true. Jörg Colberg, "A Conversation with Kai-Olaf Hesse," *Conscientious Extended*, November 13, 2007, http://jmcolberg.com/weblog/extended/archives/a_conversation_with_kai-olaf_hesse/.

11
In a 2012 BA thesis, photographer Marcin Klimek dissects the complexity and paradoxes of the deadpan genre, concluding that while deadpan is commonly defined as "distanced and emotionless," in photography it is often employed as a "form of criticism and ideological debate." Marcin Klimek, "Deadpan photography; an expressive genre and an invitation to the discussion. A call for new definition," BA Honors thesis, Edinburgh Napier University, 2011, https://issuu.com/bintphotobooks/docs/10.1.1.456.4675.

12
Terry Munro, *Empire of Illusion* (London: Black Dog Press, 2017), 11.

13
Ada Louise Huxtable, "Living with the Fake, and Liking It," *New York Times*, March 30, 1997, https://www.nytimes.com/1997/03/30/arts/living-with-the-fake-and-liking-it.html.

14
"Prehistoric Park," *Dinny's Digest* (Calgary: Calgary Zoological Society, 1983): 5. Emphasis added.

15
Ibid.

skillfully concealed, pipes and hoses removed from view, and the landscape filled out with lush greenery and flowing water features. Paired with the earlier photographs, these pictures provide a visual record of the evolution of a highly contrived "natural" landscape. While there are hints that this is a site for human interaction, such as a discreet fence lining a small pond and a walking path that leads through a stone archway (fig. 47), to an undiscerning eye there is little to suggest that this is a man-made place. Here, the simulacrum is on full display and one must suspend critical faculties to read the landscape as one entirely designed and built by human hands. The relationship between the before and after photographs is, therefore, a complex one; while the land appears improved, its artifice is also cast in high relief.

In the introduction to *Empire of Illusion*, Munro's book of Las Vegas pictures, curator and writer Bill Jeffries writes that Munro's use of black and white film "addresses the dilemma of portraying the subject of his critique without further glamorizing it."[12] He suggests that the absence of color gets at the "reality" of place and works in opposition to Sin City's visual excessiveness. A similar outcome is achieved in Munro's *Mesozoic Park* photographs. In black and white the pictures fail to capture the rich brown tonal variations of hoodoos or the deep green hues of plant life, thereby denying the pleasure of gazing at the spectacle. Greyscale instead favors surface texture, emphasizing the painstaking detail that went into the creation of this counterfeit reality. With an aesthetic of the banal, Munro refuses to glamorize the attraction but insists instead on its hollowness. The photographs bring to mind a quote from the late architecture critic Ada Louise Huxtable, who, in an opinion piece on the state of artificiality in America, wrote that "the surrogate version is rarely sublime; more often it is a reduced and emptied-out idea based on what [André] Corboz has called the 'poverty of the re-invention of the not known'."[13] Perhaps the greatest irony of the Prehistoric Park is that it is located little more than 100 km away from the Alberta Badlands, the province's richest fossil-bearing deposits and a landscape closest to one that existed 65 million years ago. While an exceedingly impressive natural environment exists a stone's throw away from the city of Calgary, the commodified, surrogate landscape of the Prehistoric Park is still considered an acceptable—and, for many, a preferred—experience.

When the Prehistoric Park re-opened in the 1980s, the Calgary Zoo did not shy away from advertising its artifice. In fact, the Park was celebrated as both a scientific and creative triumph, and the designers and construction crews were applauded for their skill in creating such a remarkable simulation. According to an article published on the occasion of the Park's unveiling, "the purpose of the new prehistoric park is to display *scaled-down* portions of the landscape of Western Canada as they *may have appeared* during the Mesozoic Era."[14] The article comments on the horticultural challenge of imitating jungle-like vegetation that no longer exists nor could withstand the cooler climate of present day, as well as the artistic license used in the Prehistoric Park's overall design. Hoodoos, for example, were included as a visual barrier and sound berm, offering protection from vehicular traffic bordering the Park. While the presence of hoodoos during the Mesozoic Era is "questionable," their inclusion here is justified by their close association with the rich fossil region of the nearby Badlands.[15] Realism is thus compromised in favor of widely held assumptions about the Earth's prehistoric past. The Prehistoric Park therefore is a perfect simulacrum, a site that has no true referent. It is an amalgamation of topographies crammed into a 6.5-acre site intended to represent one of the most transformative eras of the Earth's history.

Constructed in the early 1930s, the original Prehistoric Park included life-sized models of a variety of extinct animals, a panoramic time tunnel, and a fossil house. By the mid 1970s, when the dinosaur models began to show their age and were forced to compete with the zoo's live animal collection, a major renovation was undertaken to move, expand, and modernize the park. With the goal of realism, aging dinosaur models were swapped out for fewer new ones and the gardens were expanded and updated to heighten the illusion. Earthmoving equipment was used to put massive boulders in place and sculptors were employed to shape the geological features, spraying them with gunite concrete, and finishing with colored plaster intended to replicate the various rock strata of the Mesozoic Era.

These renovations represent a shift in cultural understandings of scientific knowledge as manifested in zoological design. Architectural historian Rachel Couper maintains that zoos are a mechanism in the formulation of knowledge: "The design [of a zoological garden] is a consequence of human interpretations of the way in which the natural world should be perceived and presented. Zoological architecture is therefore the physical embodiment of cultural understandings of scientific knowledge, both shaping and confirming social constructions of knowledge of the natural world."[16] First emerging in the twelfth century as a collection of exotic animals for admiration and entertainment, the courtly menagerie was transformed in the late nineteenth-century during the Age of Enlightenment into the modern zoological garden, a scientific institution for public education and conservation. Cramped cages were replaced with larger, more naturalistic enclosures and the combination of botanical and animal collections formed the model for zoological gardens throughout Europe and North America. While the Prehistoric Park does not contain live animals, its objective is to educate and entertain through an embodied experience in nature and, like all modern zoos, it is "designed to mask the fundamentally and overwhelmingly human nature of the place."[17] Munro's photographs work to counter the effects of this architectural design, offering a glimpse of what lies behind the facade.

In an essay on then-recent revolutions in computers and biology and their ethical implications, visual culture theorist W.J.T. Mitchell calls on artists to engage with a "paleontology of the present" in an effort to understand our contemporary condition.[18] For Mitchell, photographers who use their cameras to record and critique the marks that humans have made on the planet contribute to such a paleontology. Through their images they work to produce "a history of art and nature much larger than our classic, romantic, and modern fashions."[19] In refusing to depict a typically picturesque landscape, Munro's photographs resist straightforward interpretation. Rather, through close looking, they open themselves up to myriad inquiries and emotional responses: to art historical analyses of the representation of nature; to aesthetic and formalist questions about the photographic image; to historically grounded understandings of the development of zoos and parks; and to cultural and economic interrogations of contemporary society, particularly of the desire for simulations of the real. Munro therefore cedes to Mitchell's call for a "rethinking of our current moment in the perspective of deep time.[20] In the end, however you choose to read these images their greatest success is that, in the words of Lucy Lippard, they "stop us in our tracks, magnify what has been barely visible, make us look again, analyze, rethink, [and] make connections to our own habitats."[21]

16
Rachel Couper, "Placing the Origins of the Zoo: An Architectural Analysis of the Metamorphosis of the Menagerie into the Zoological Garden," in *Proceedings of the Society of Architectural Historians 30, Open*, vol. 1 (2013): 235, https://www.griffith.edu.au/__data/assets/pdf_file/0028/349363/S04_01_Couper_Placing-the-Origins-of-the-Zoo.pdf.

17
Nigel Rothfels, *Savages and Beasts: The Birth of the Modern Zoo* (Baltimore & London: The Johns Hopkins University Press, 2002), 7.

18
W.J.T. Mitchell, "The Work of Art in the Age of Biocybernetic Reproduction," Artlink (March 2002), https://www.artlink.com.au/articles/2522/the-work-of-art-in-the-age-of-biocybernetic-reprod/.

19
W.J.T. Mitchell "Painting the Sea in Carson City," in *The Altered Landscape: Photographs of a Changing Environment*, 144.

20
Mitchell, "The Work of Art in the Age of Biocybernetic Reproduction."

21
Lucy Lippard, "Neutered Landscapes," in *The Altered Landscape: Photographs of a Changing Environment*, 151.

PLATES

Plates 1 to 38
Calgary, Alberta
1982

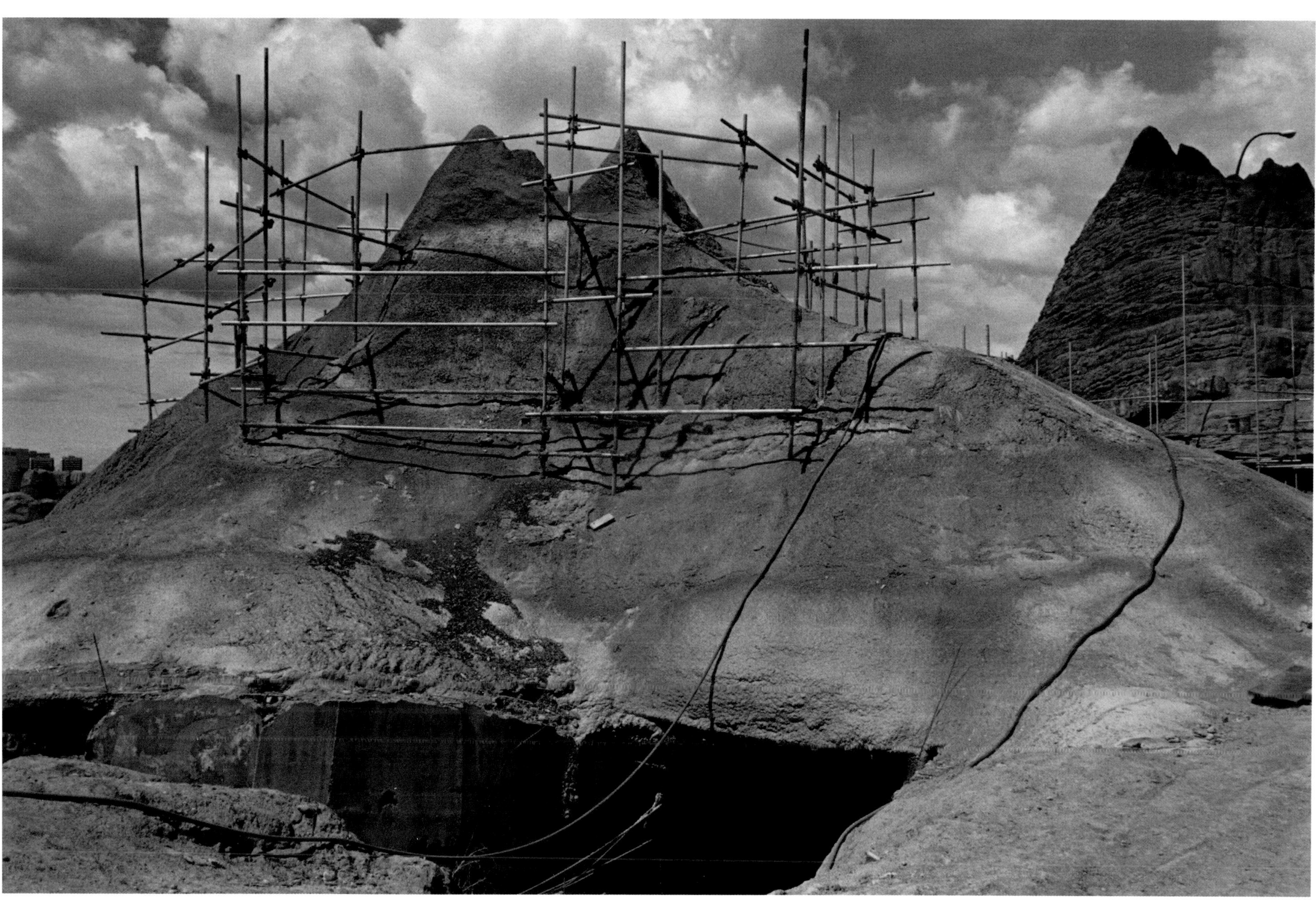

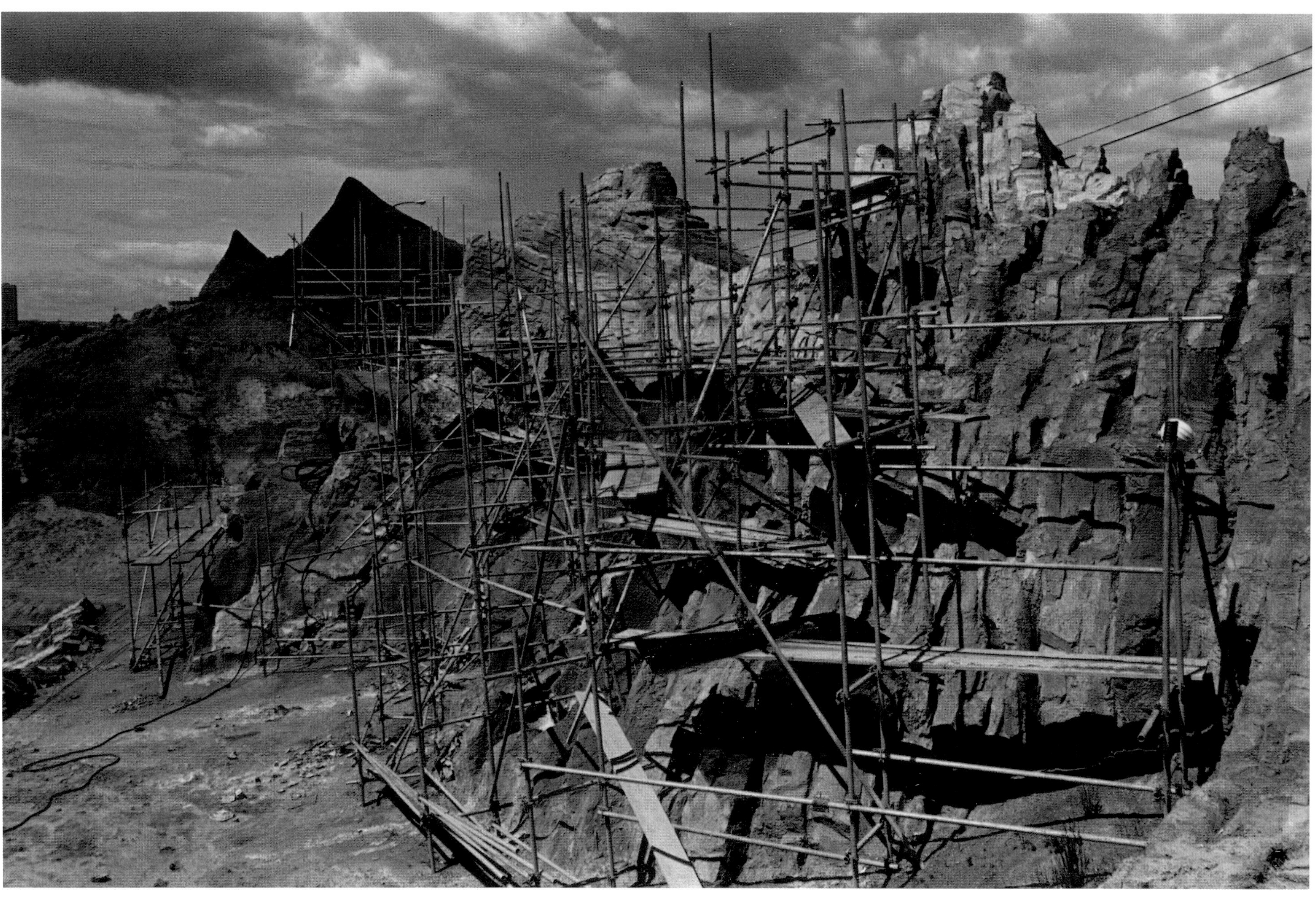

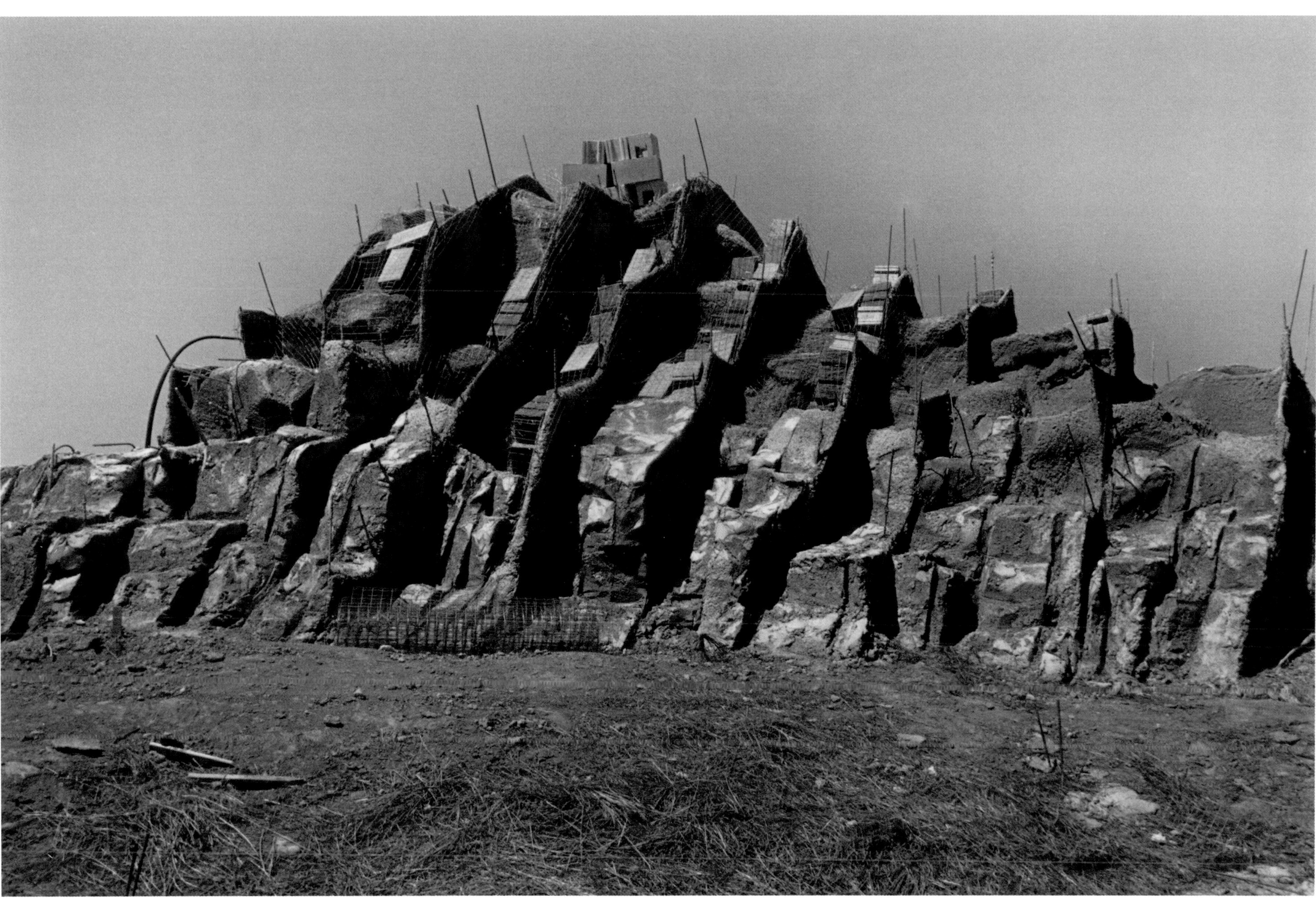

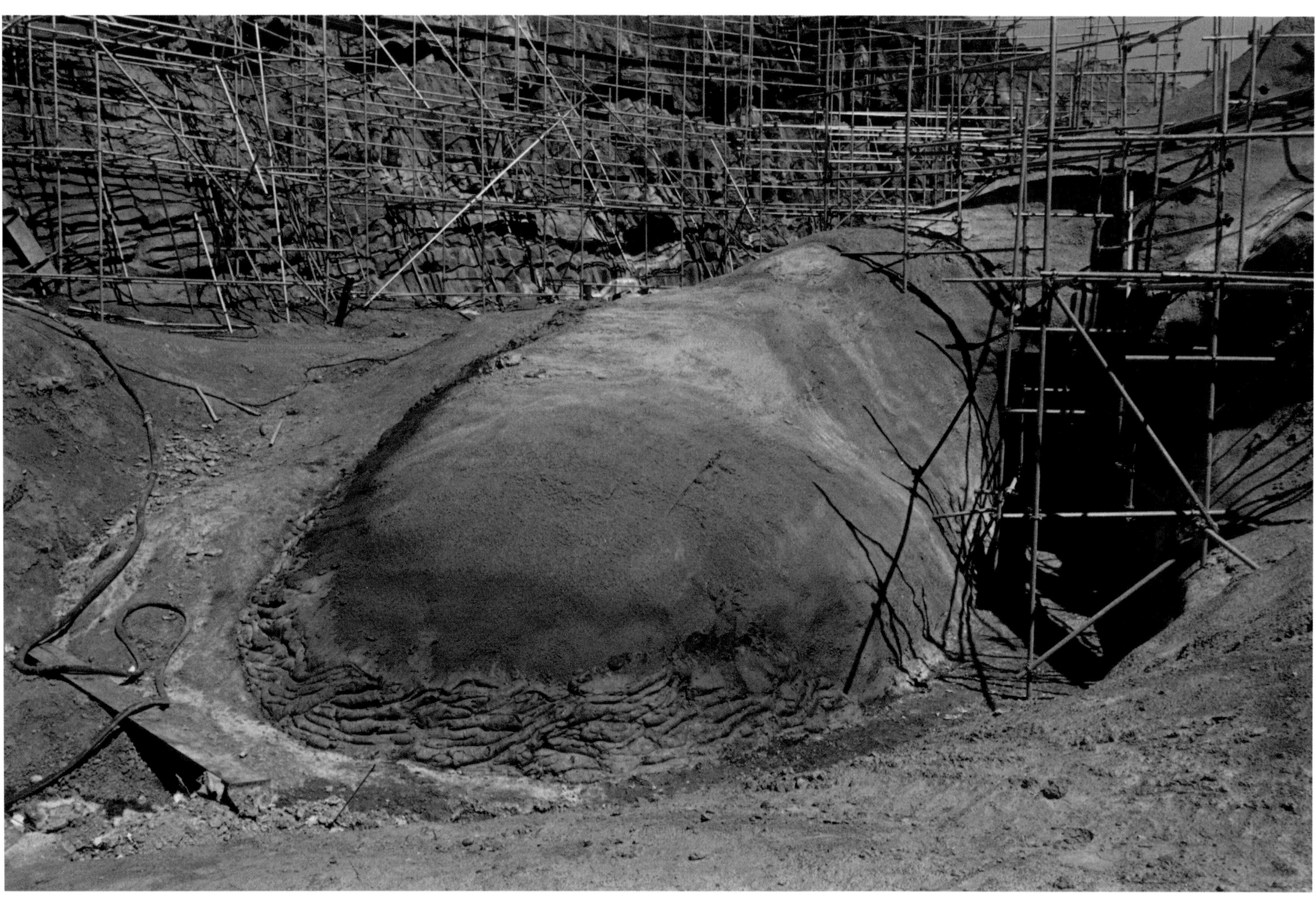

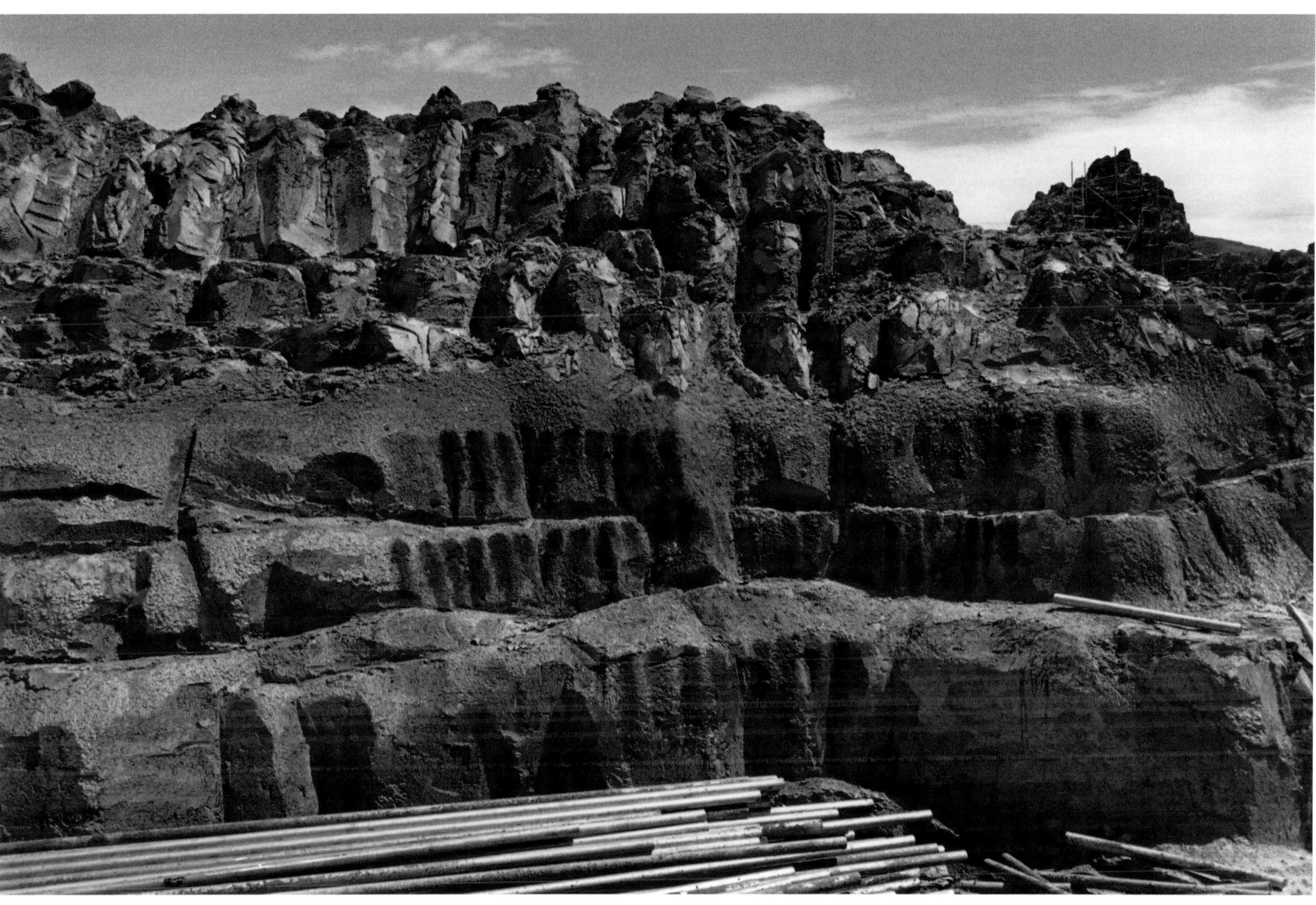

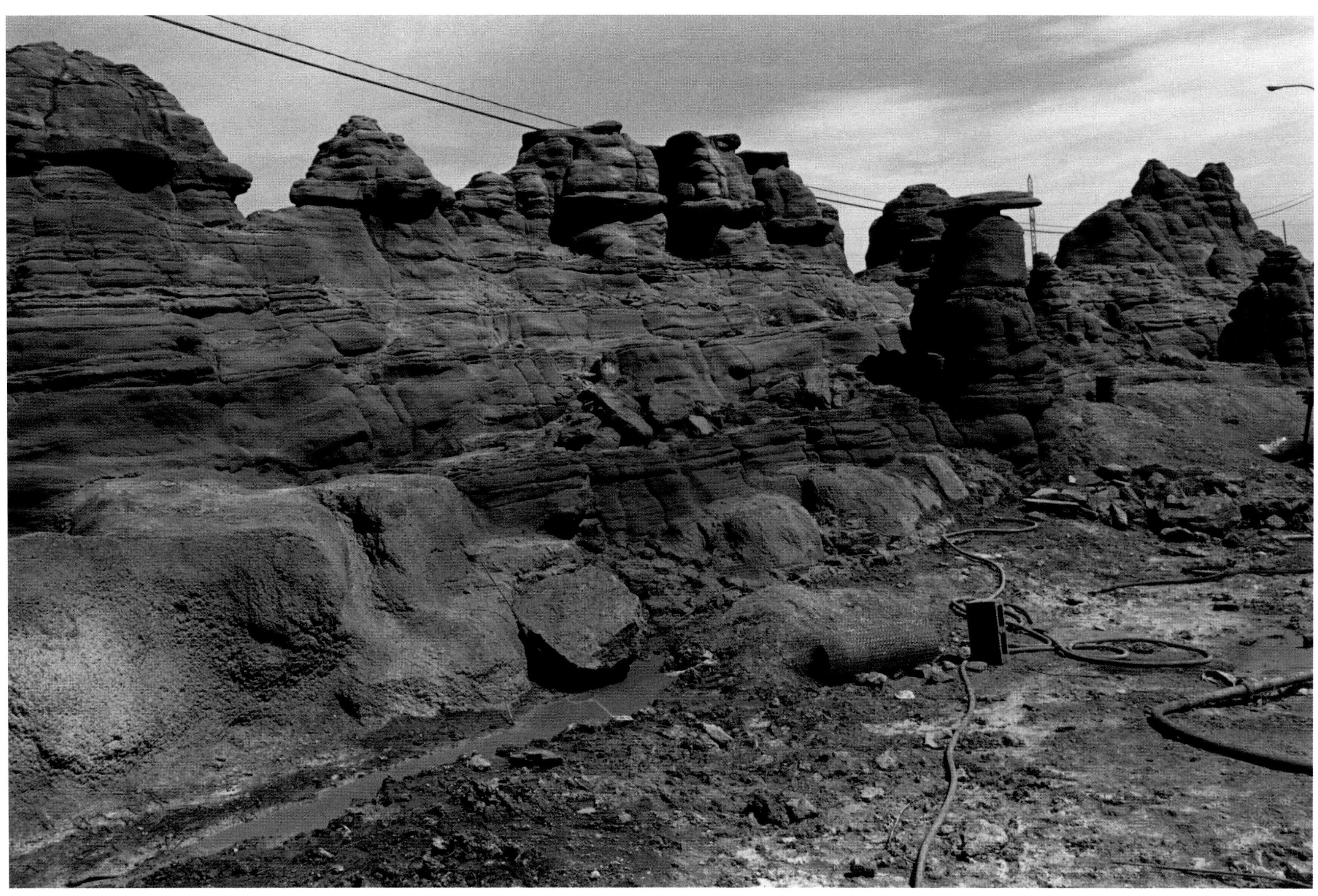

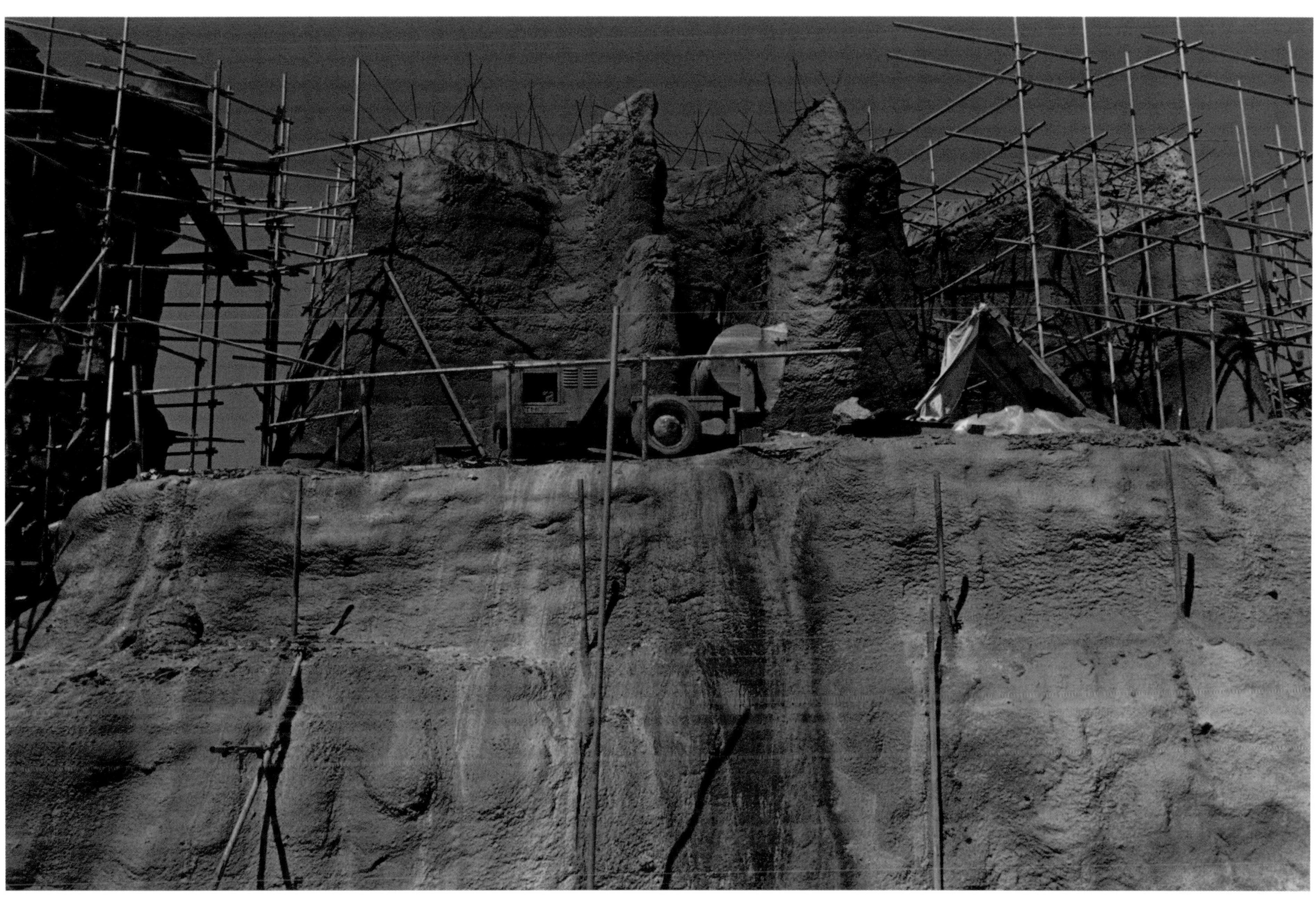

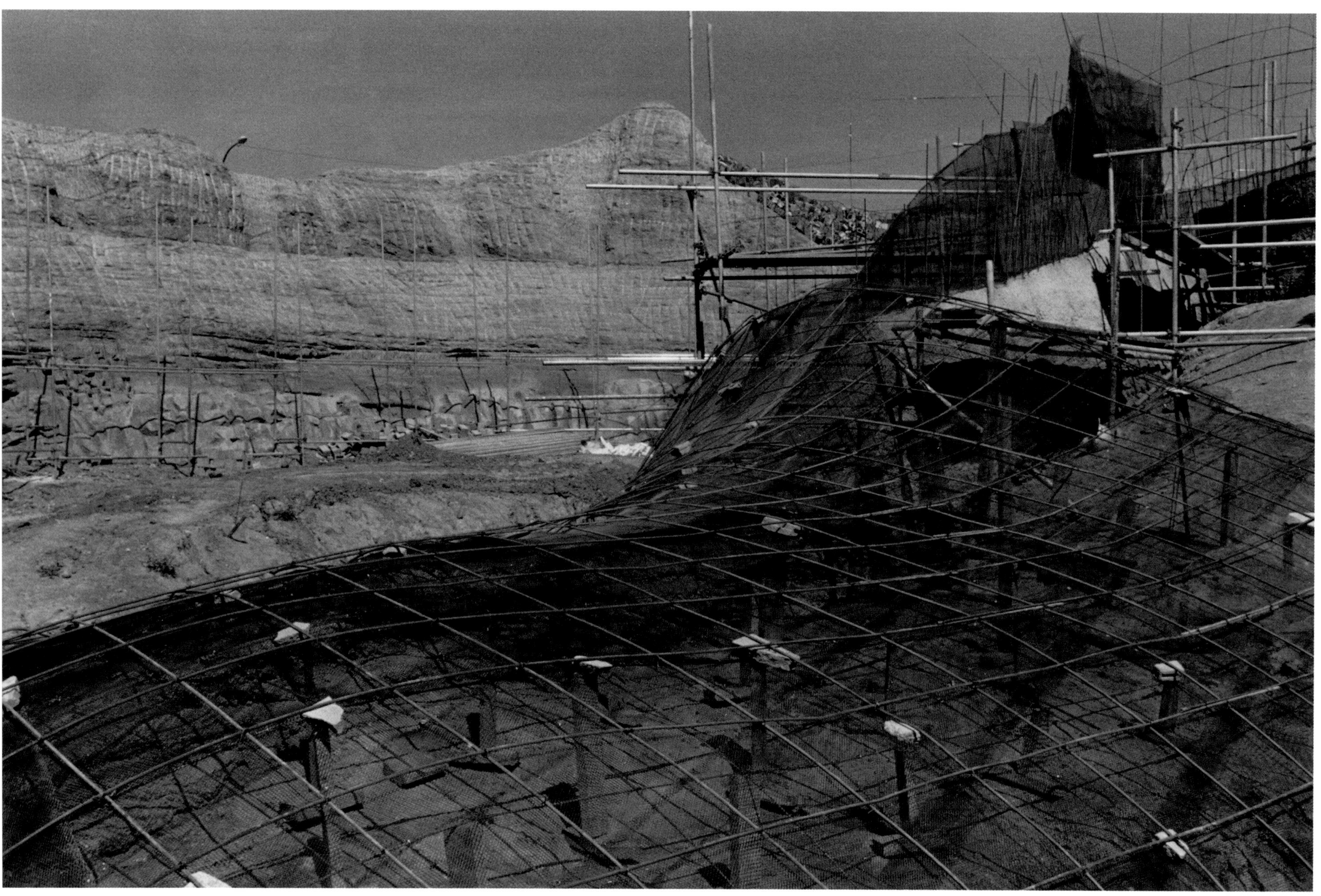

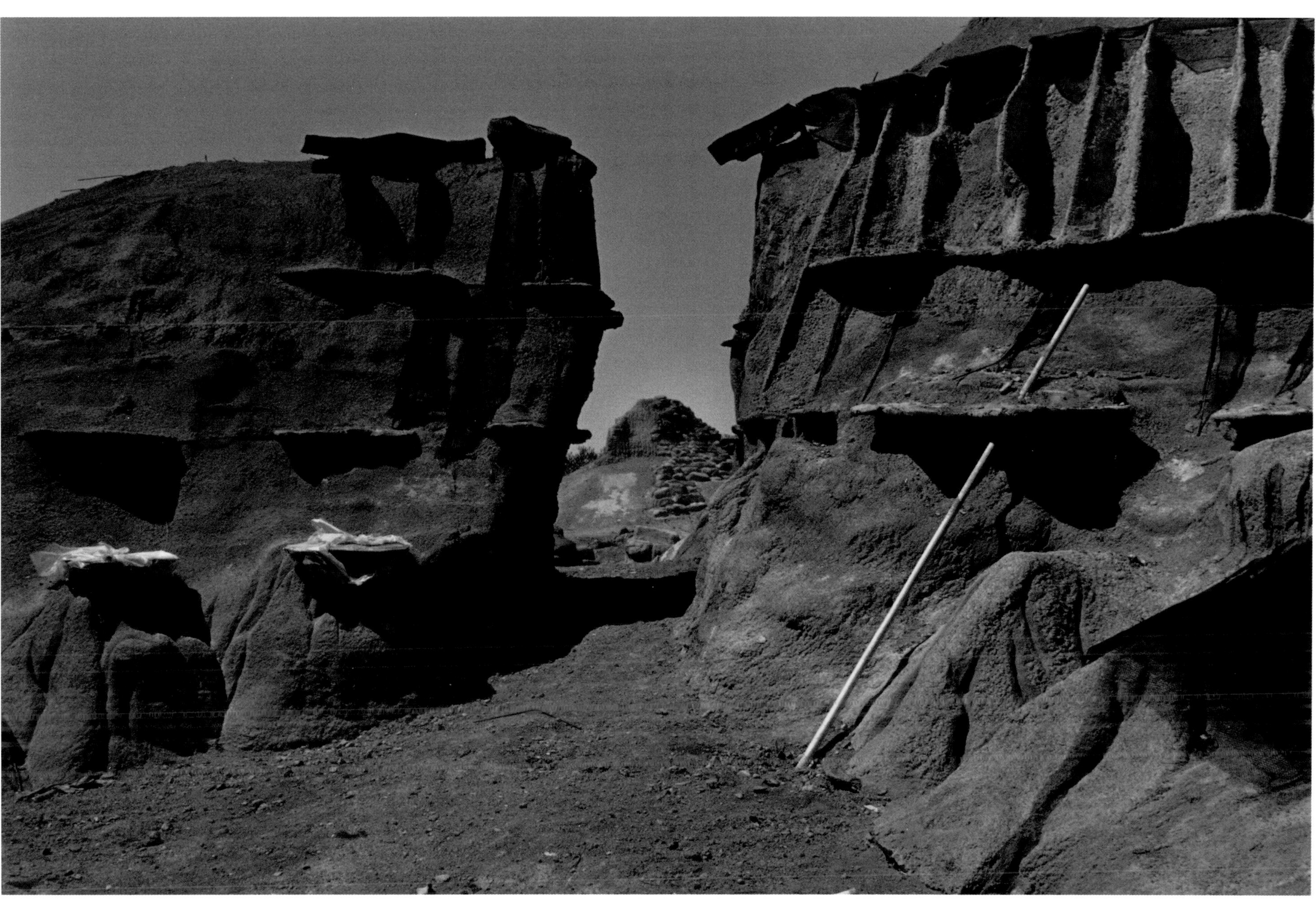

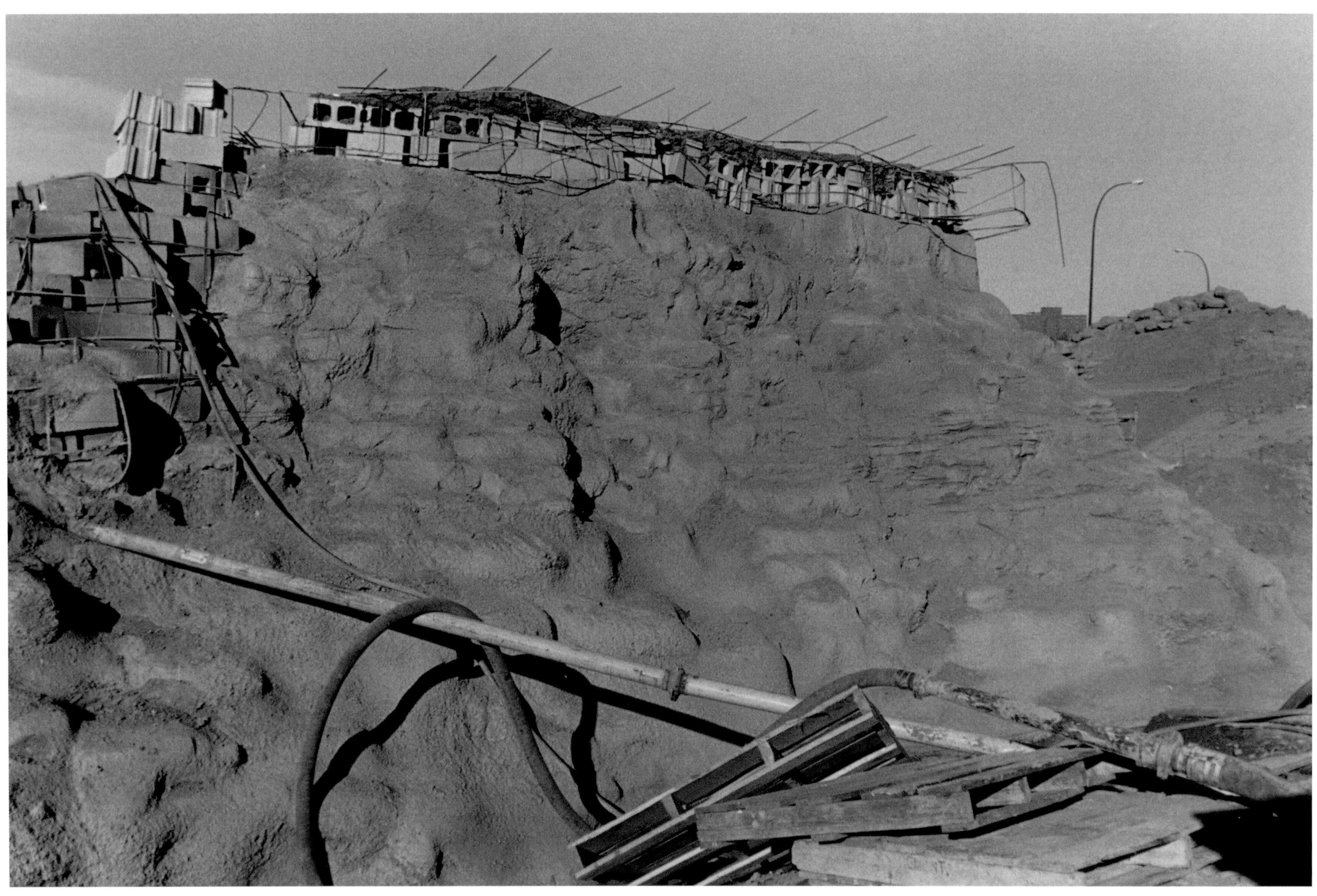

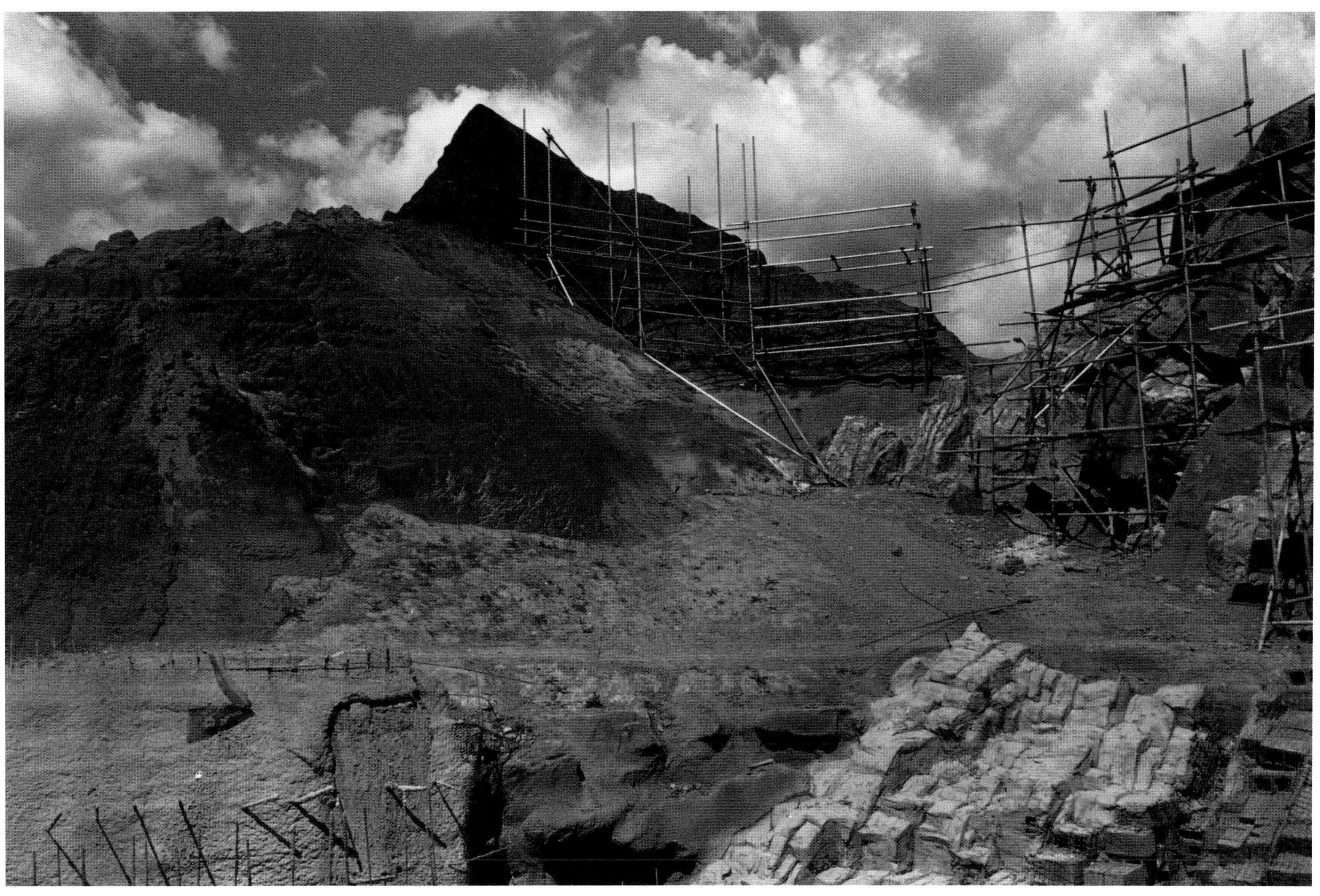

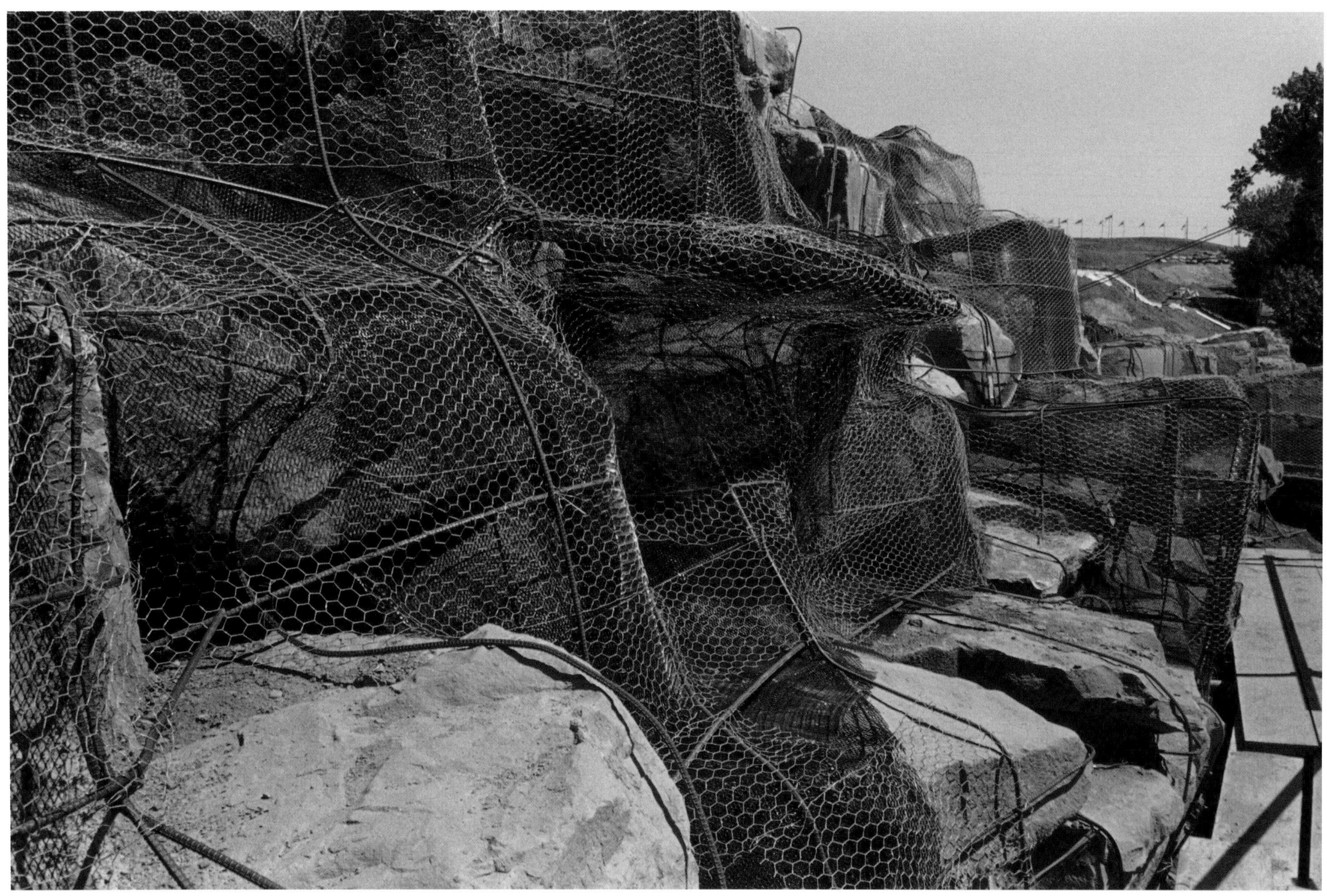

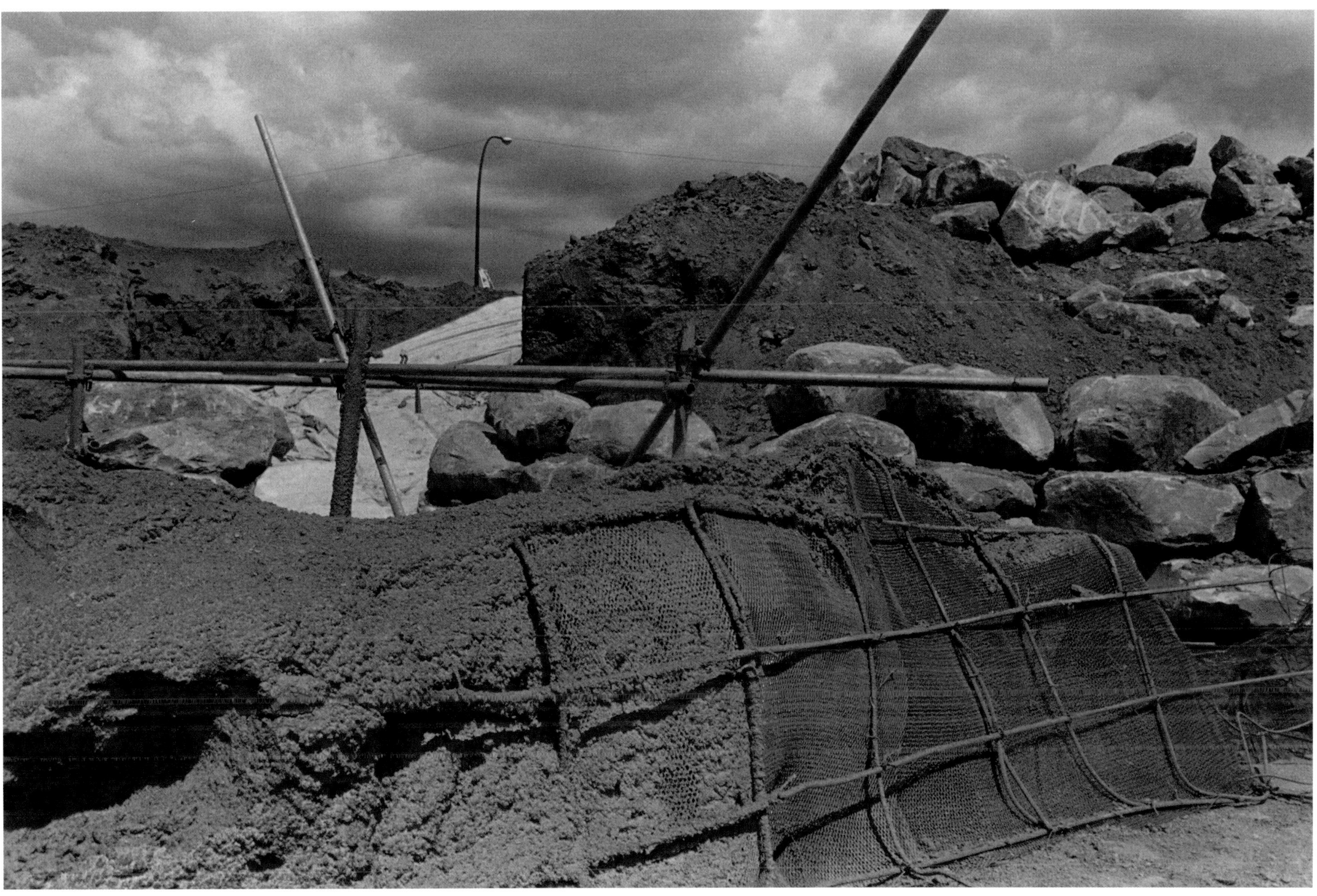

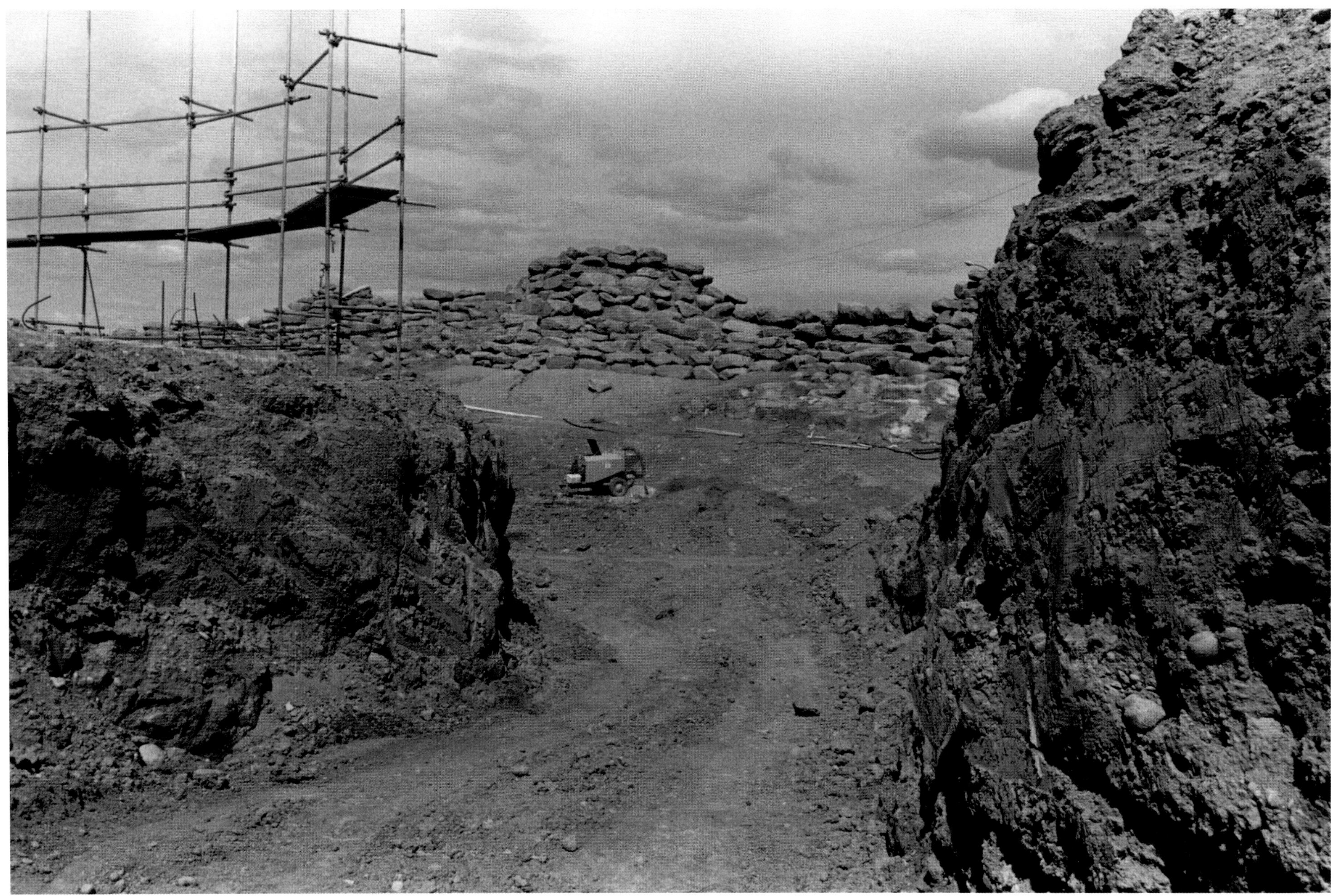

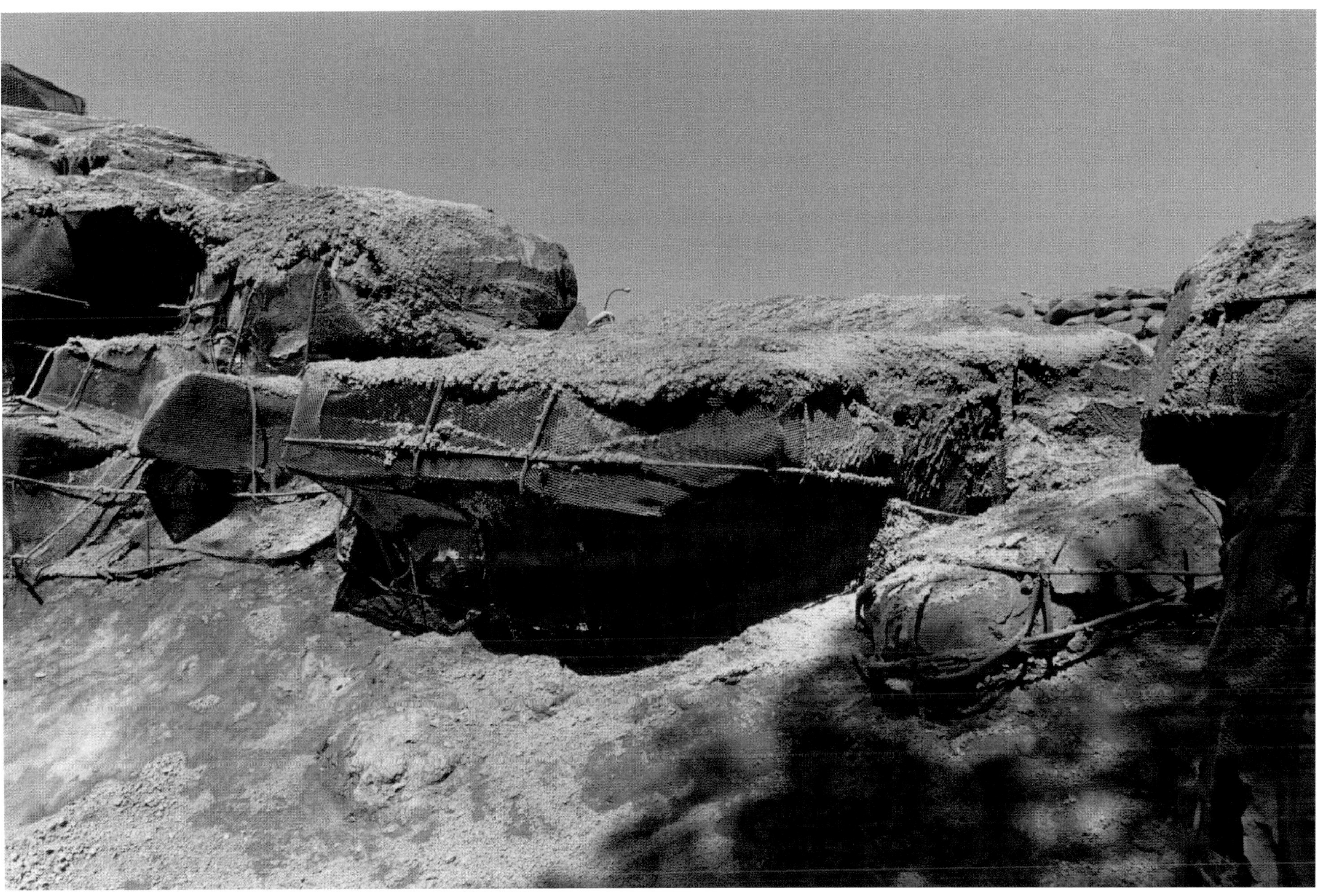

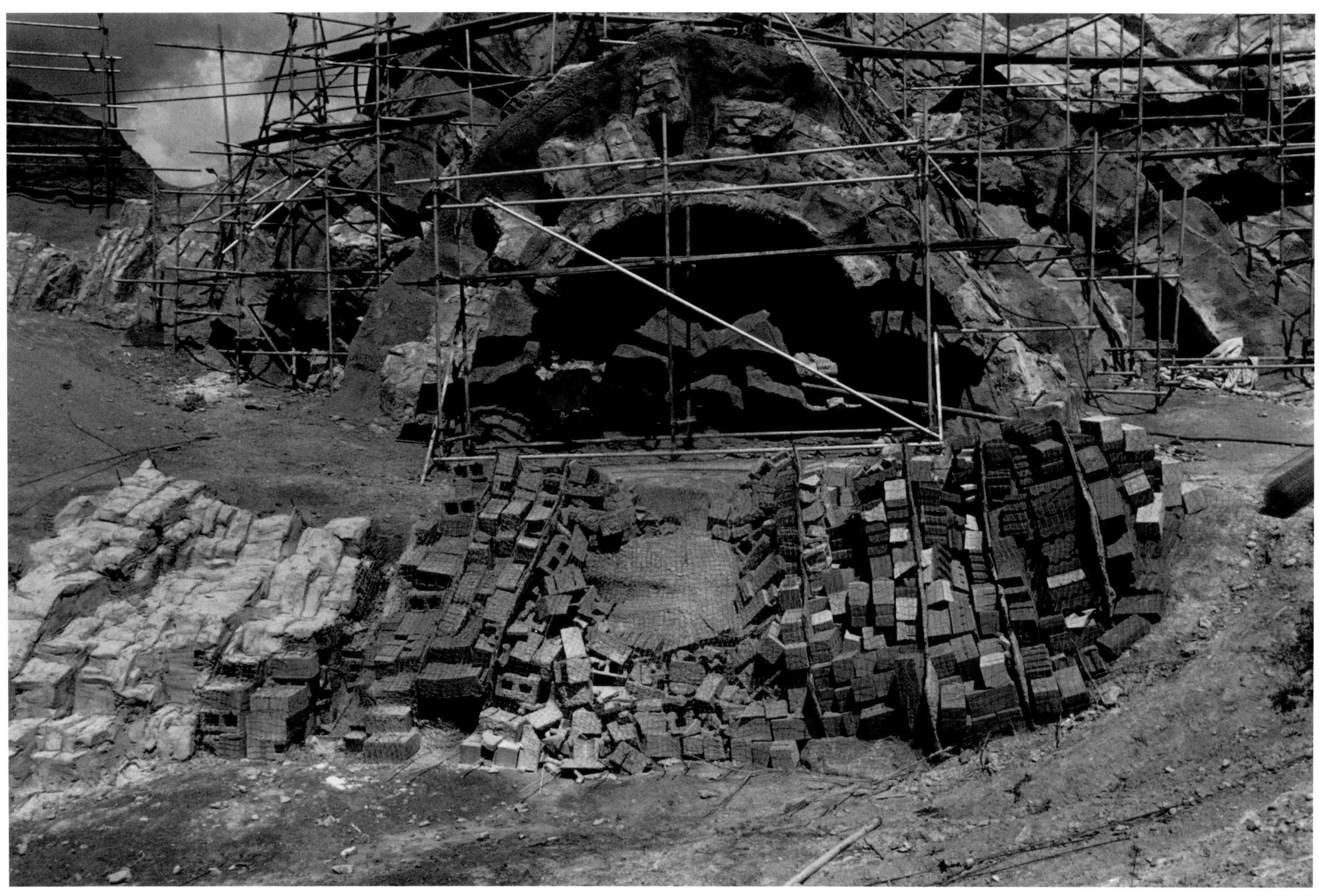

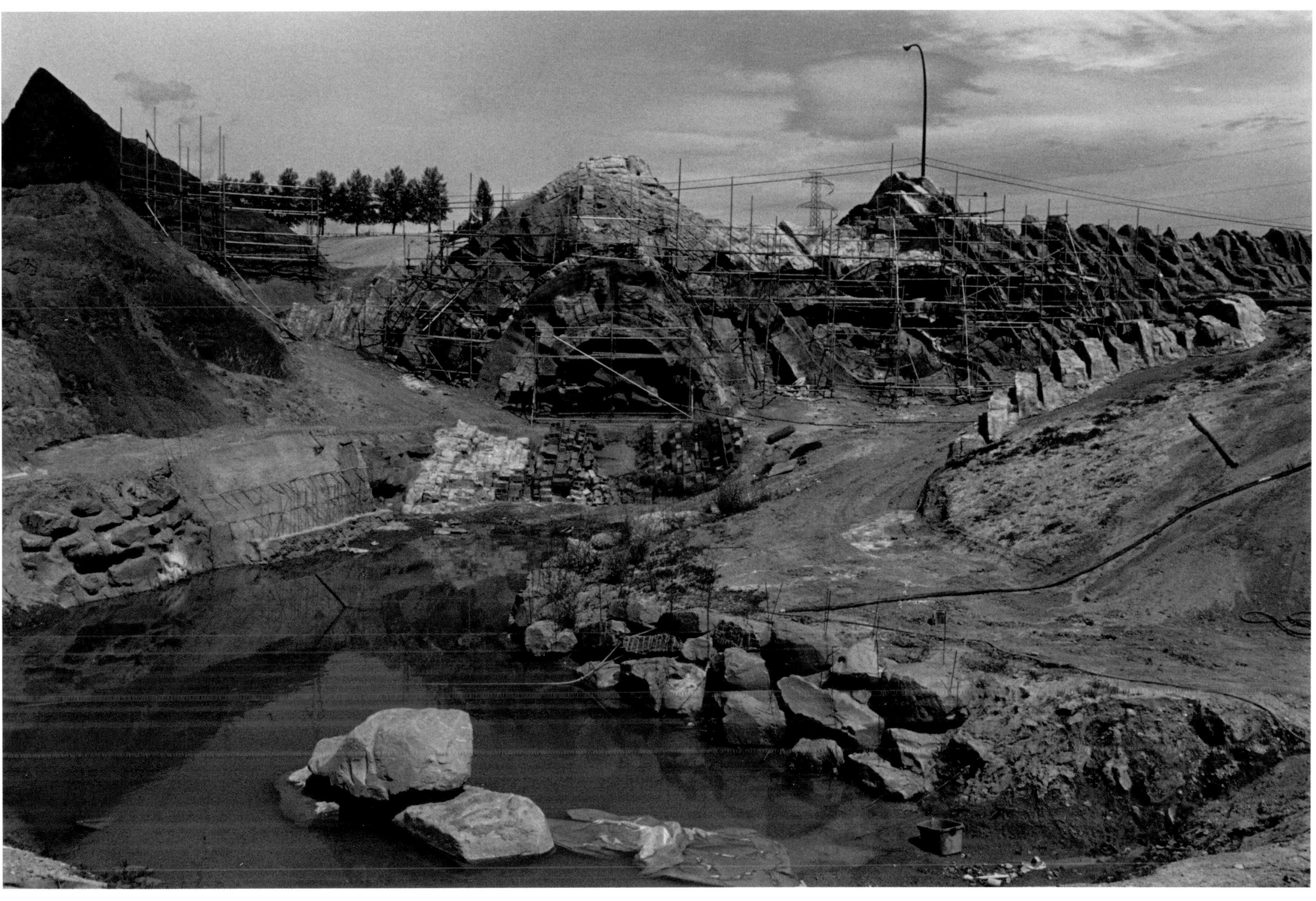

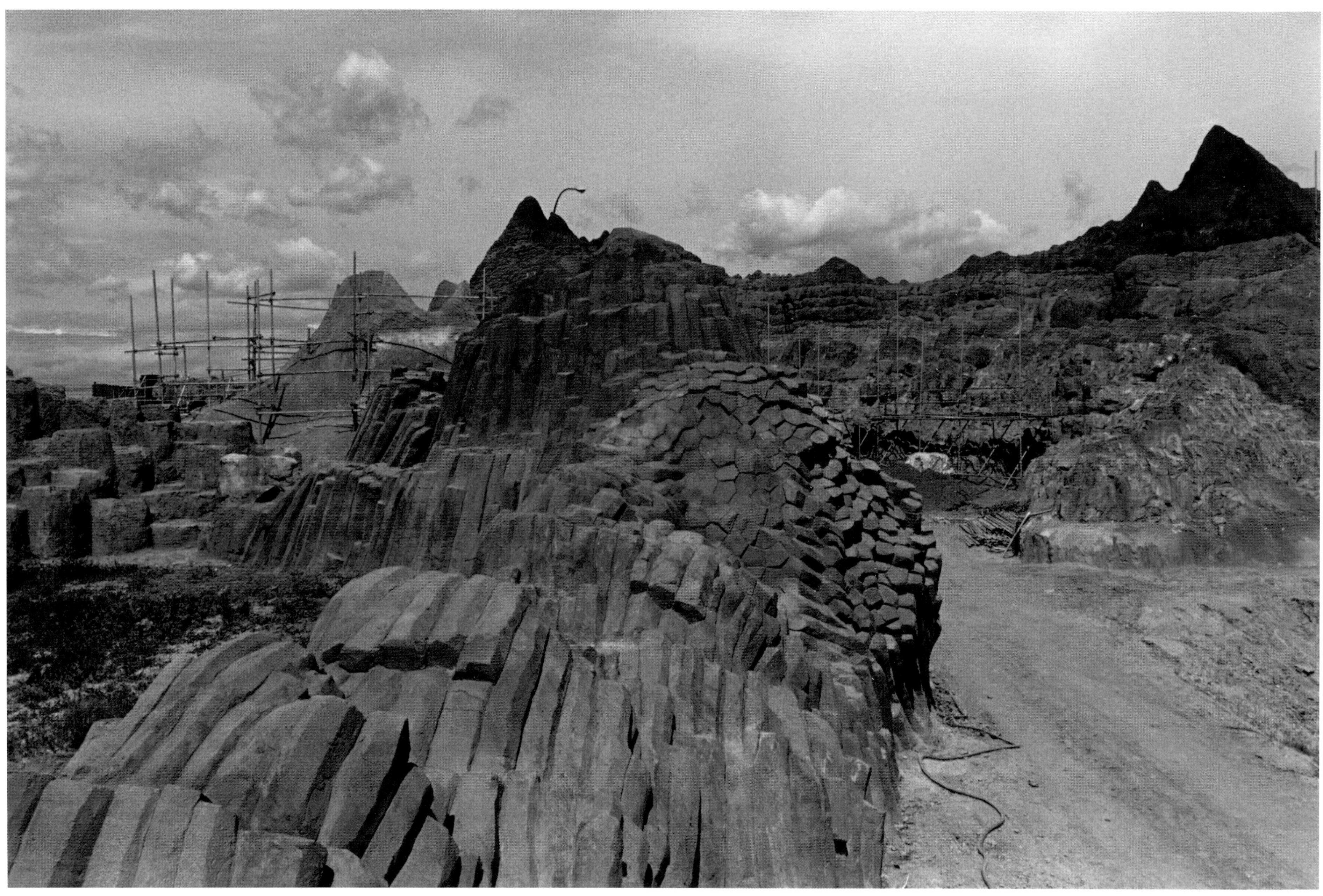

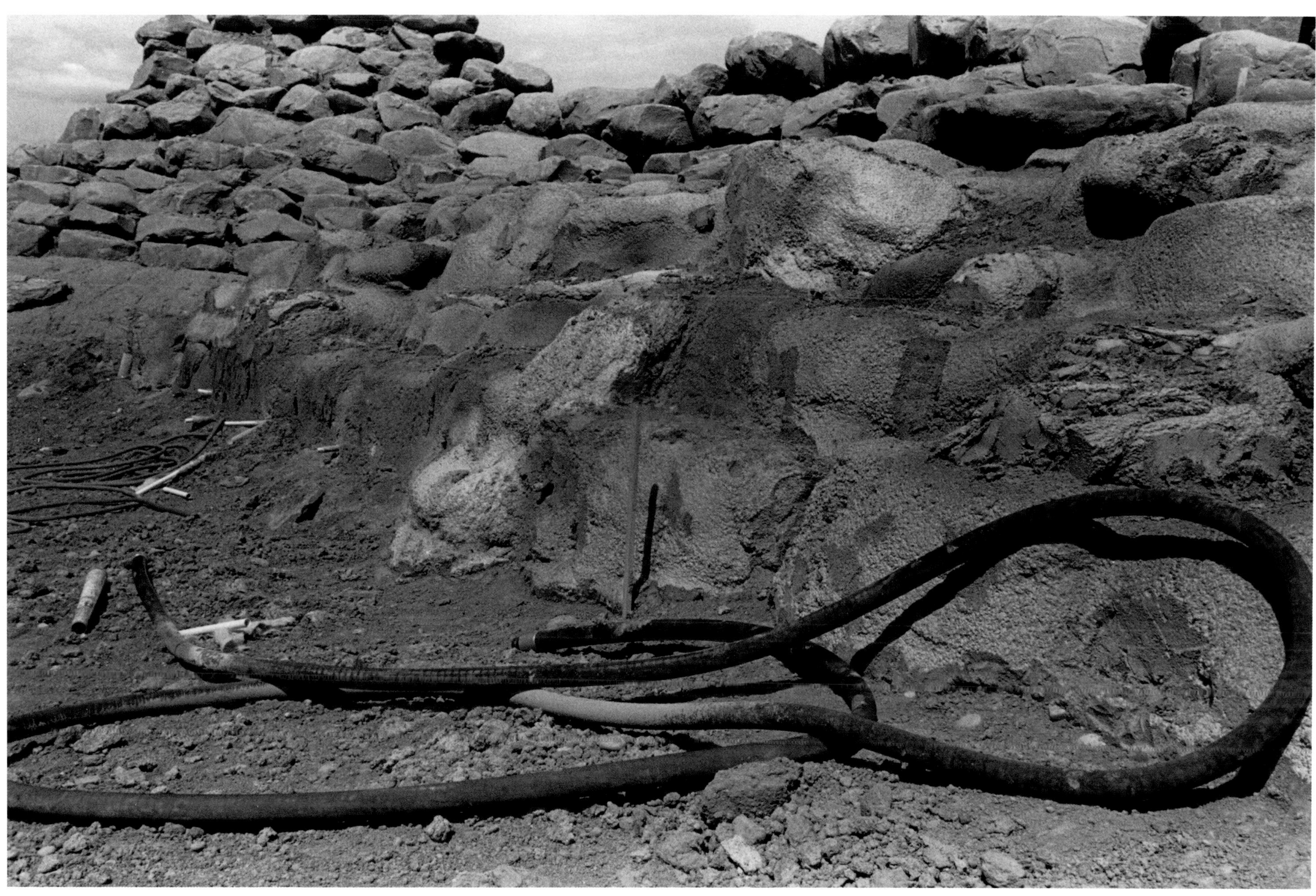

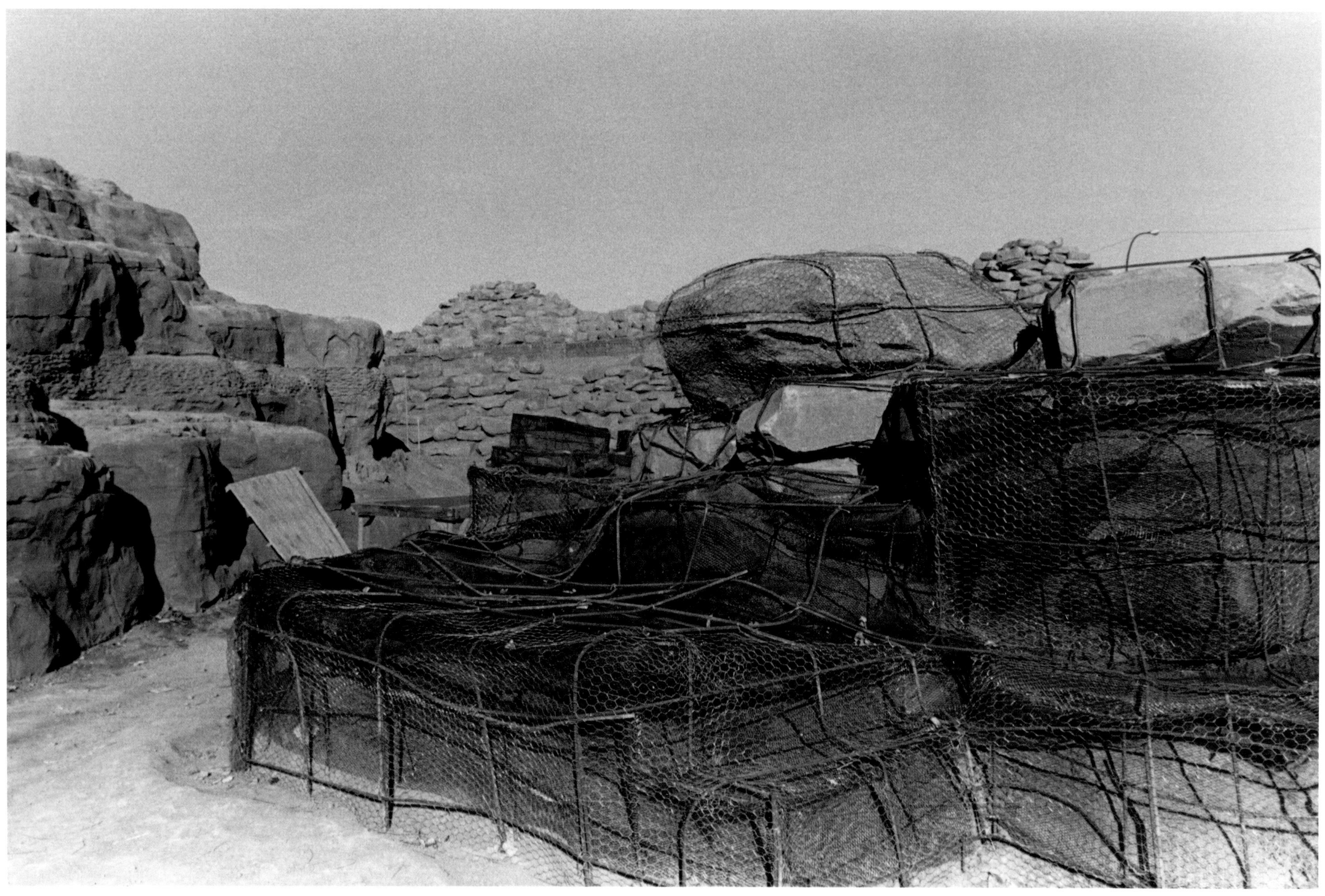

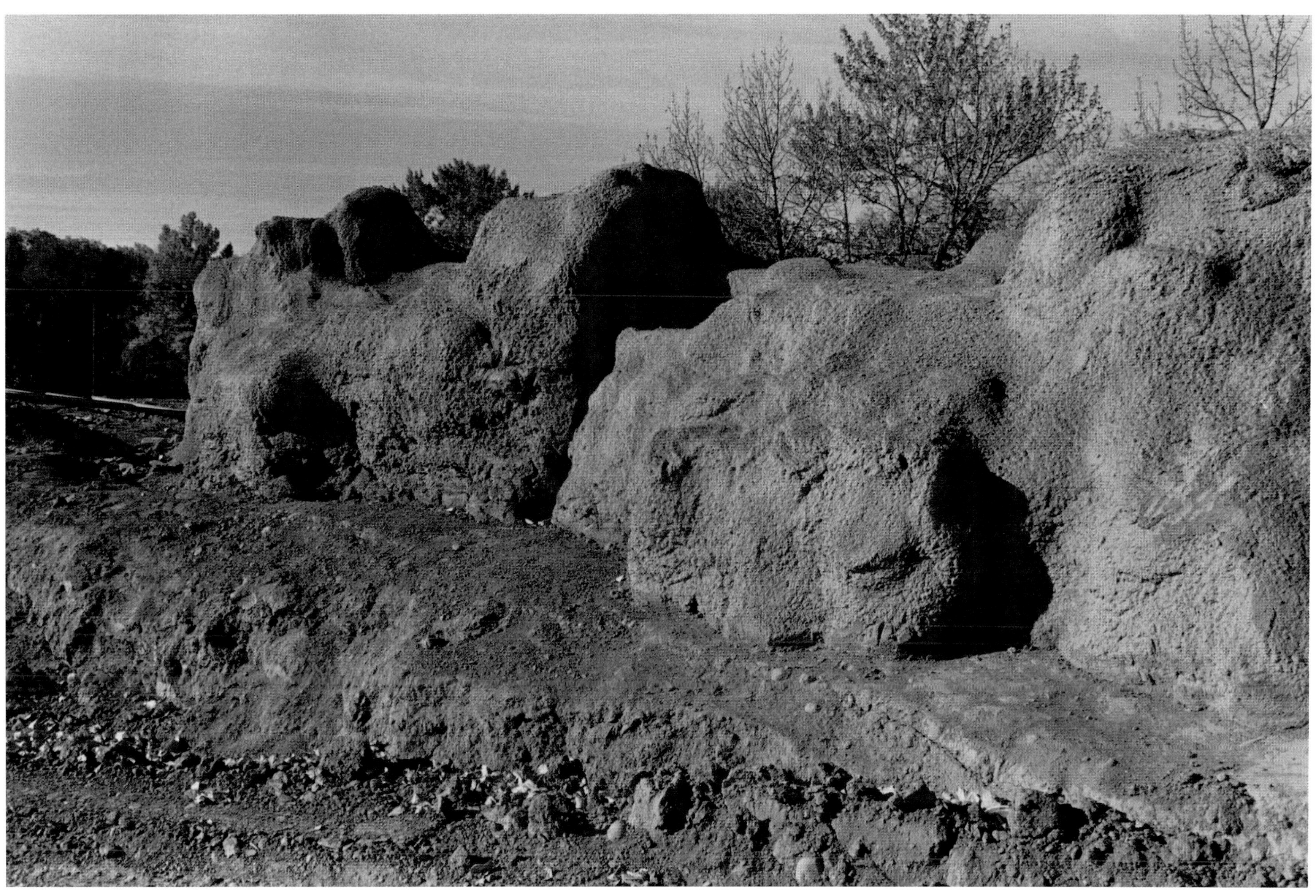

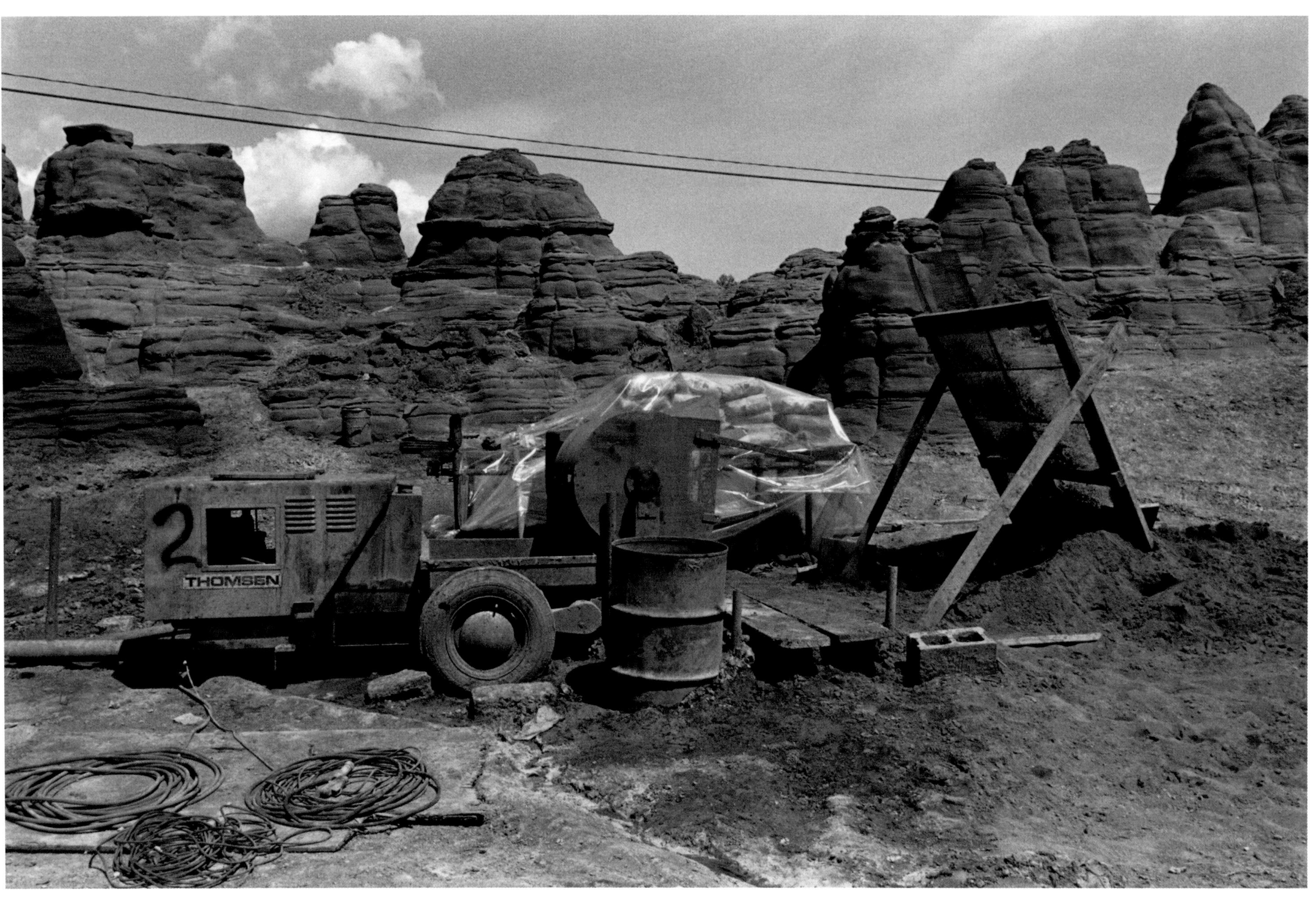

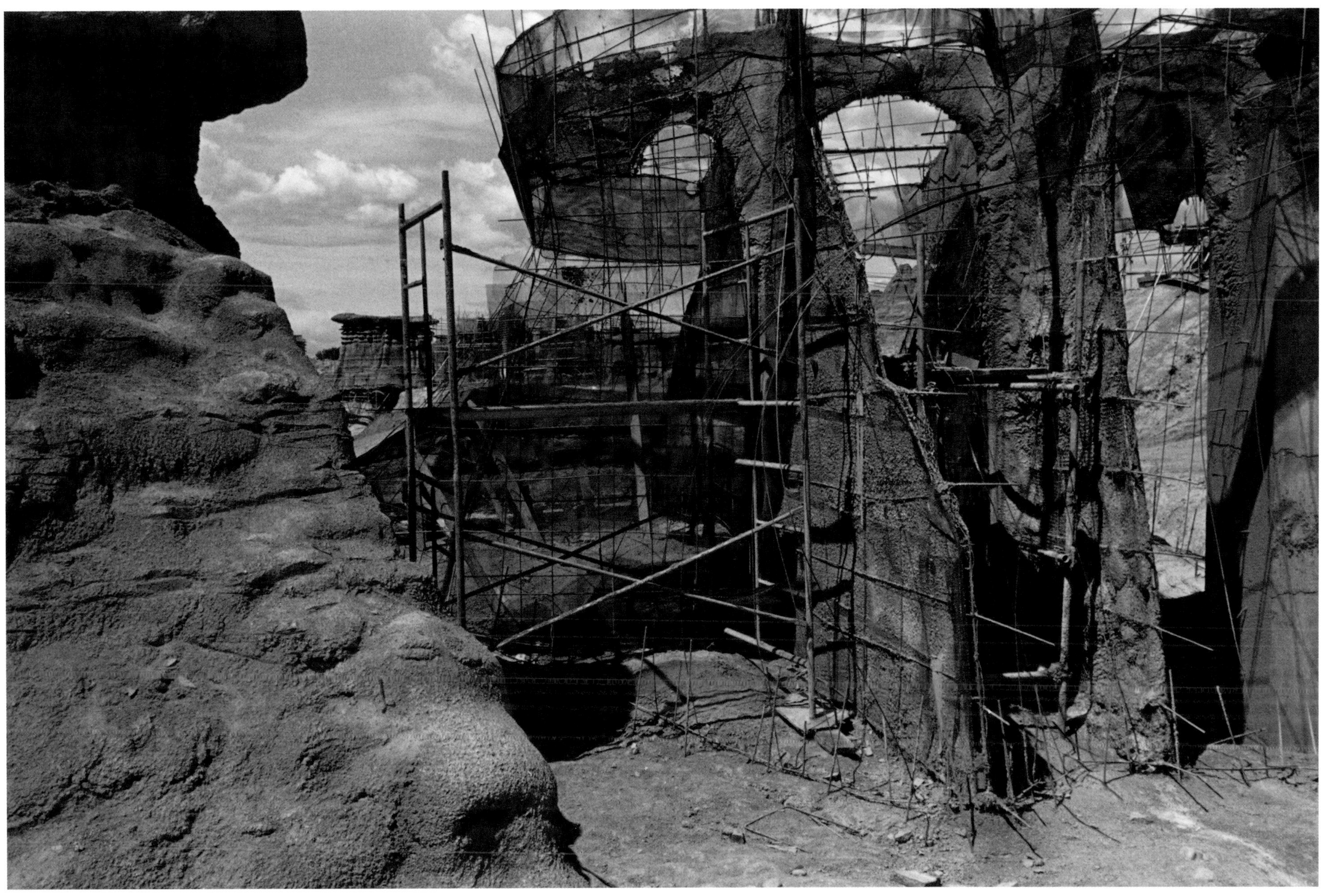

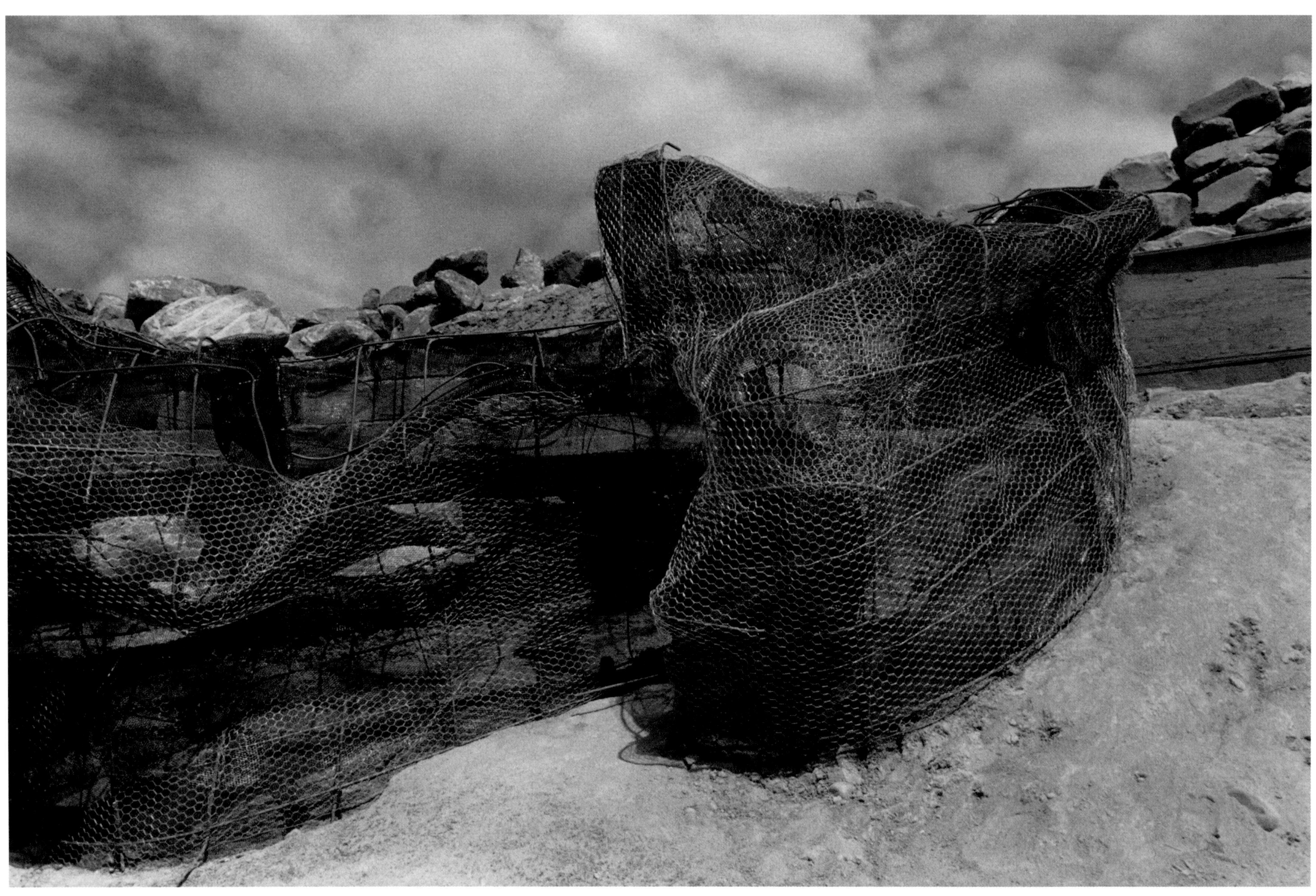

24

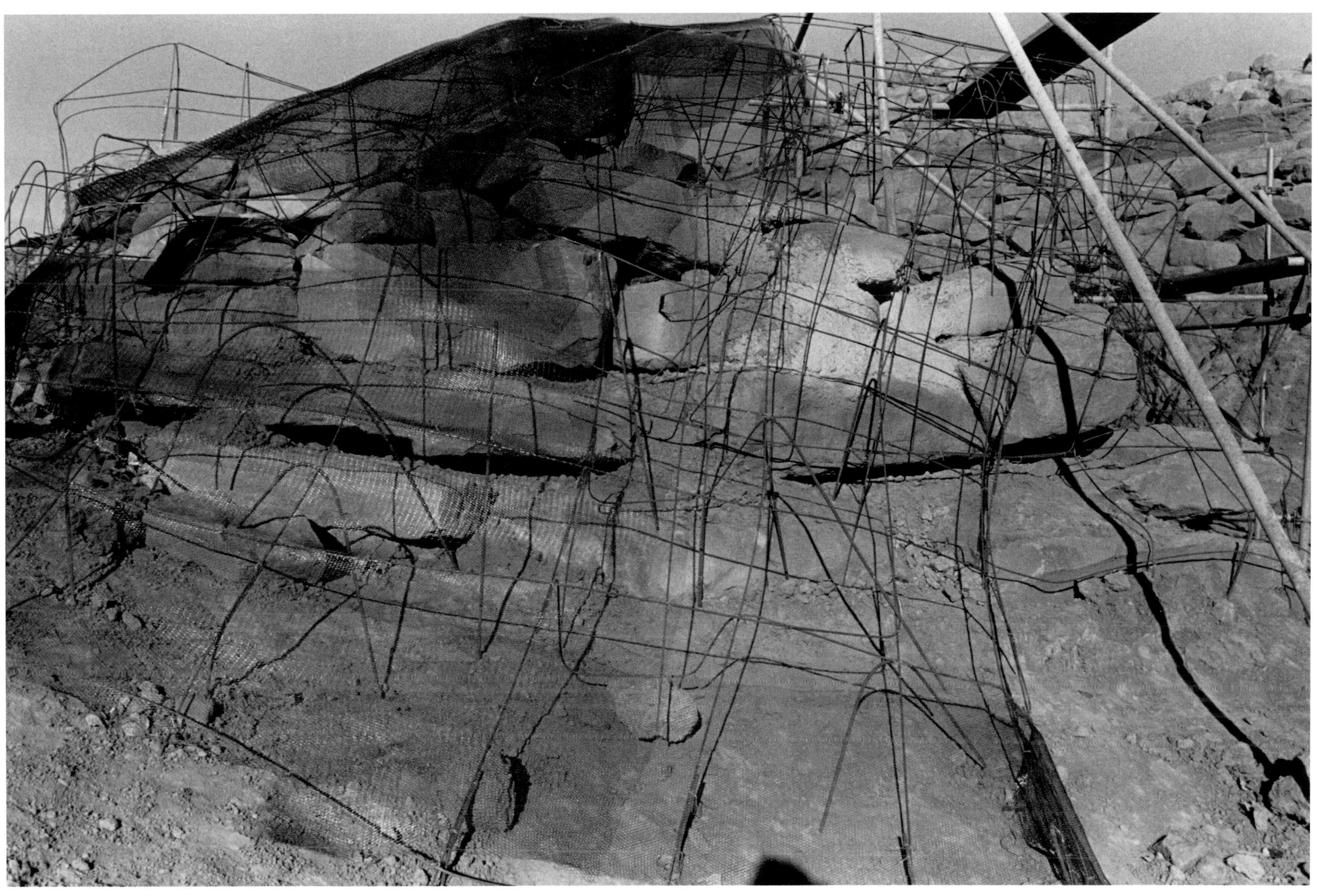

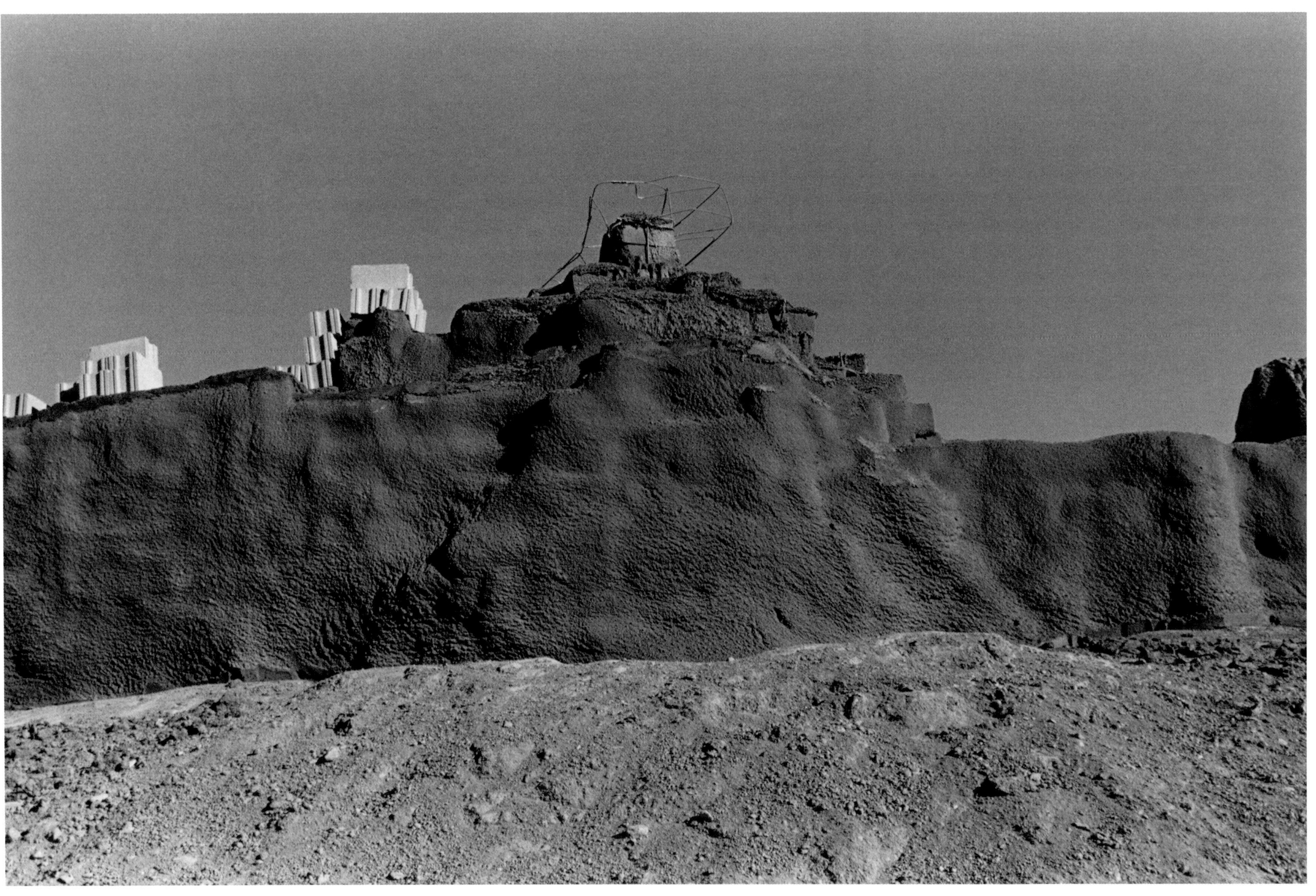

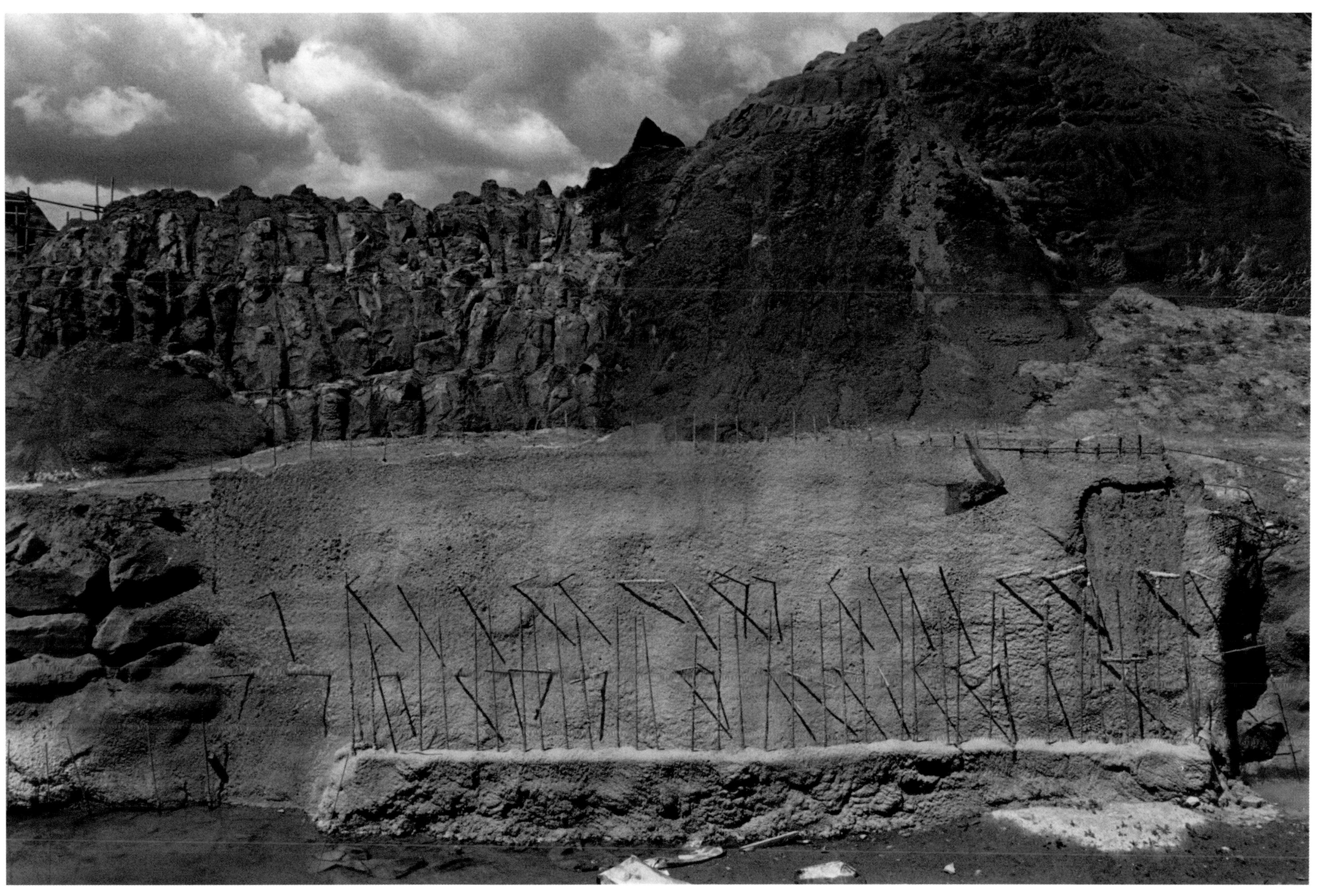

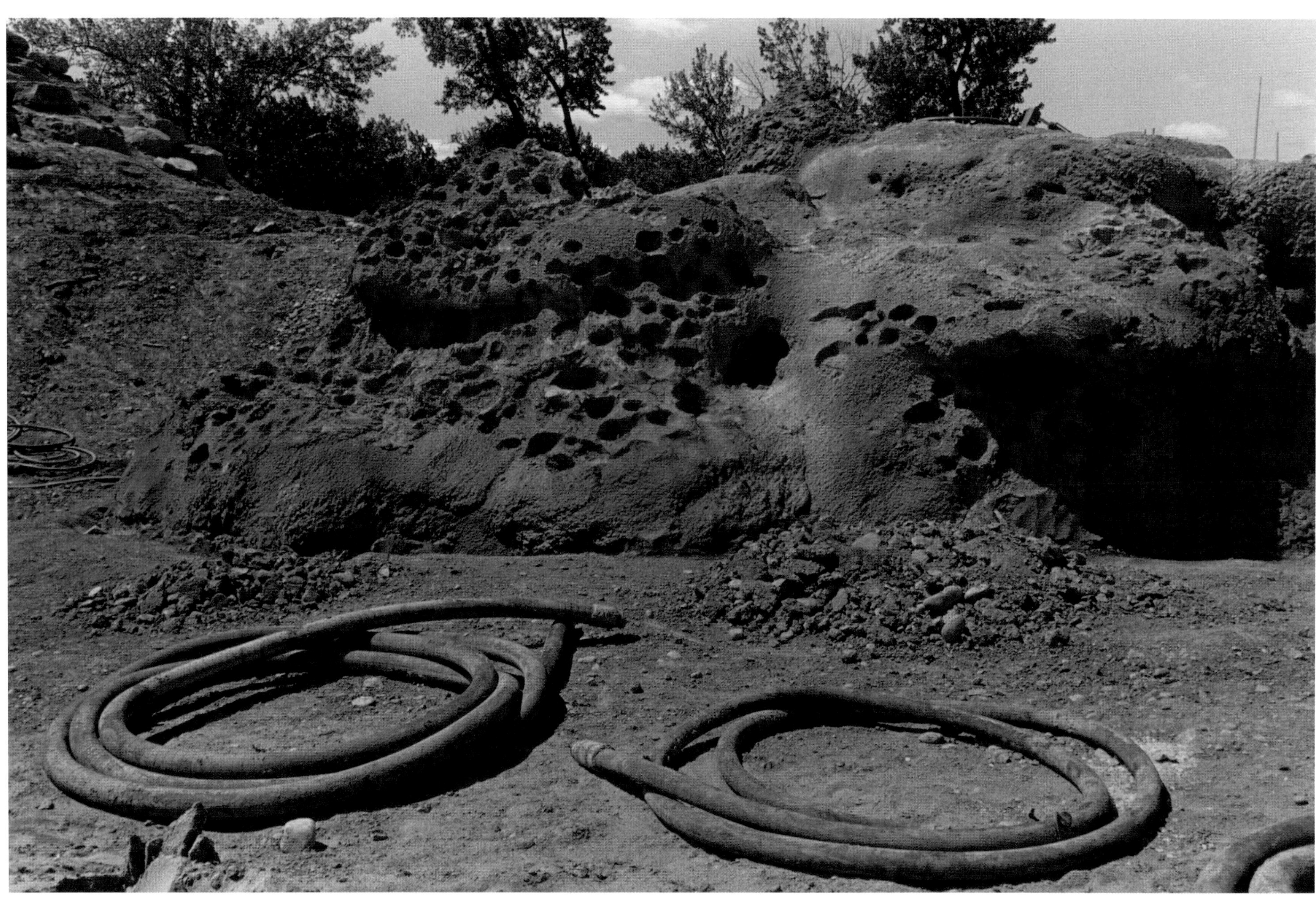

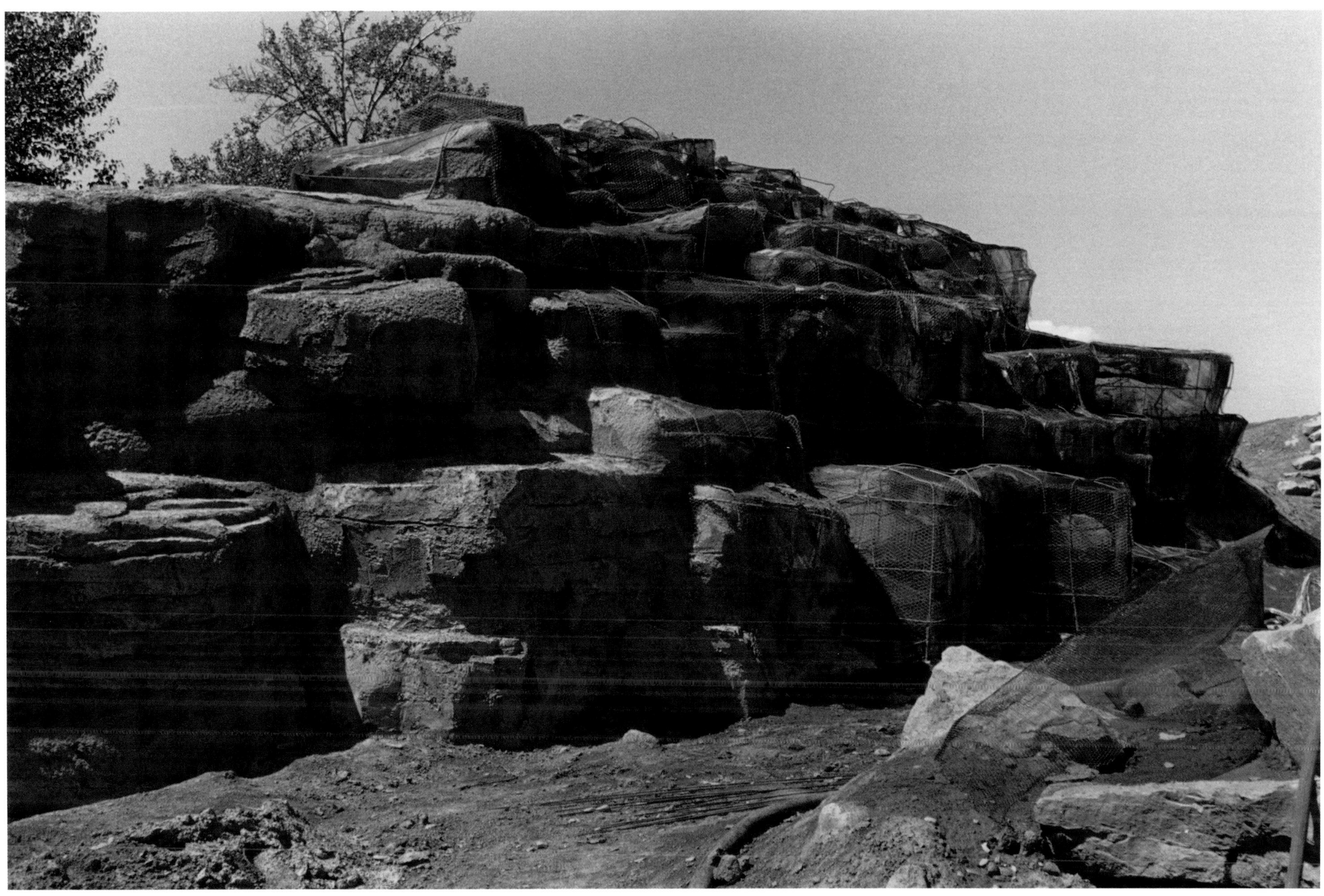

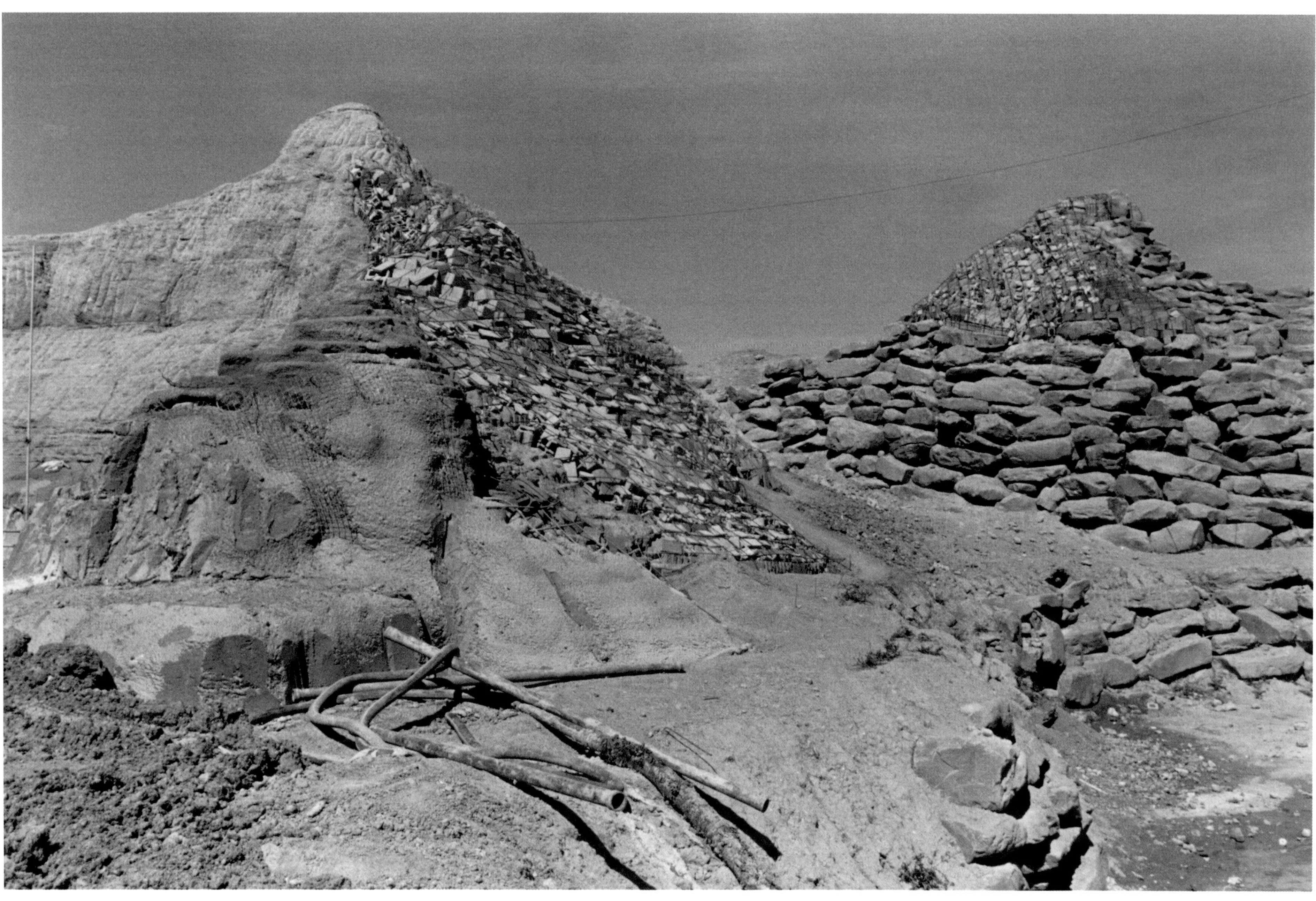

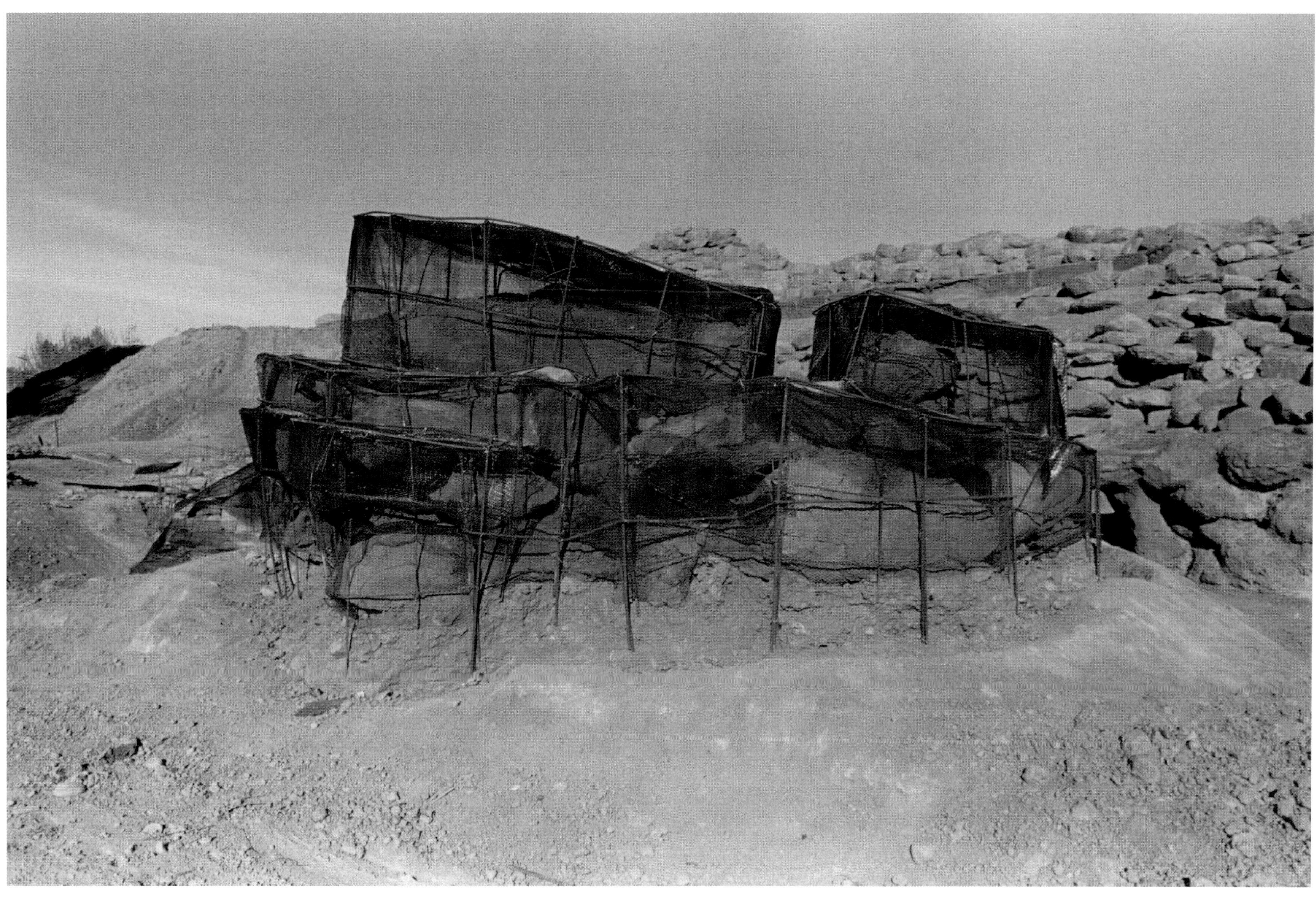

31

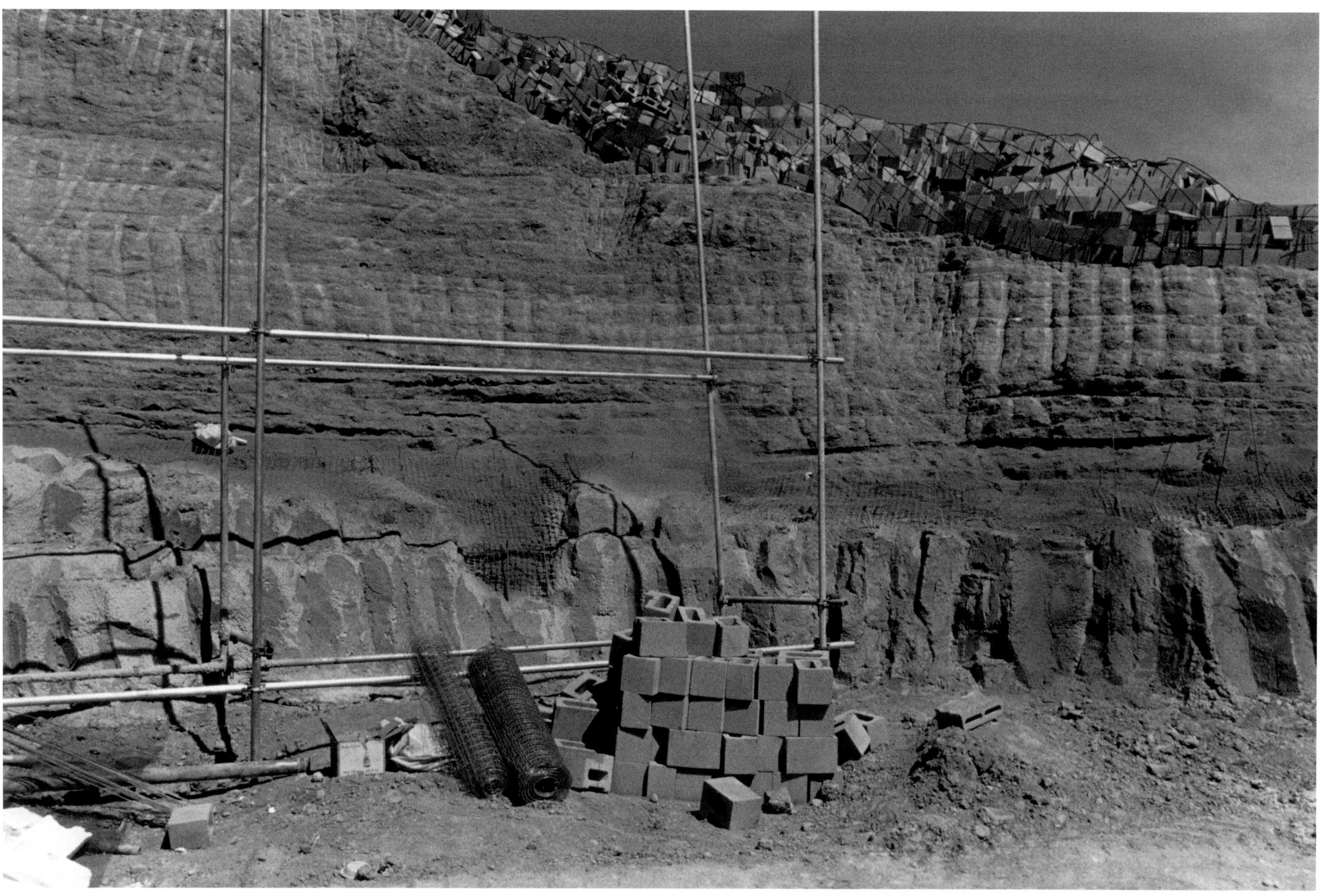

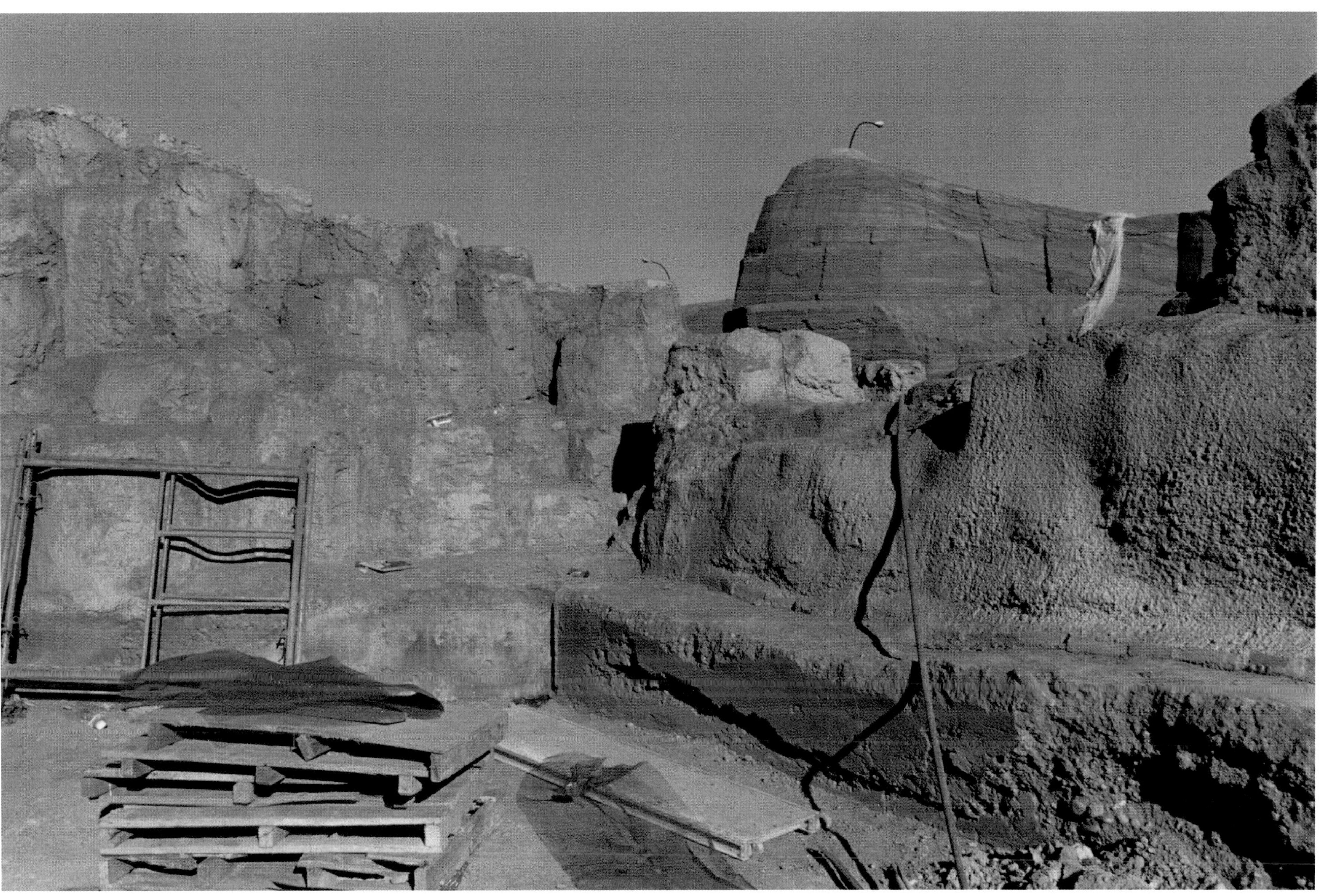

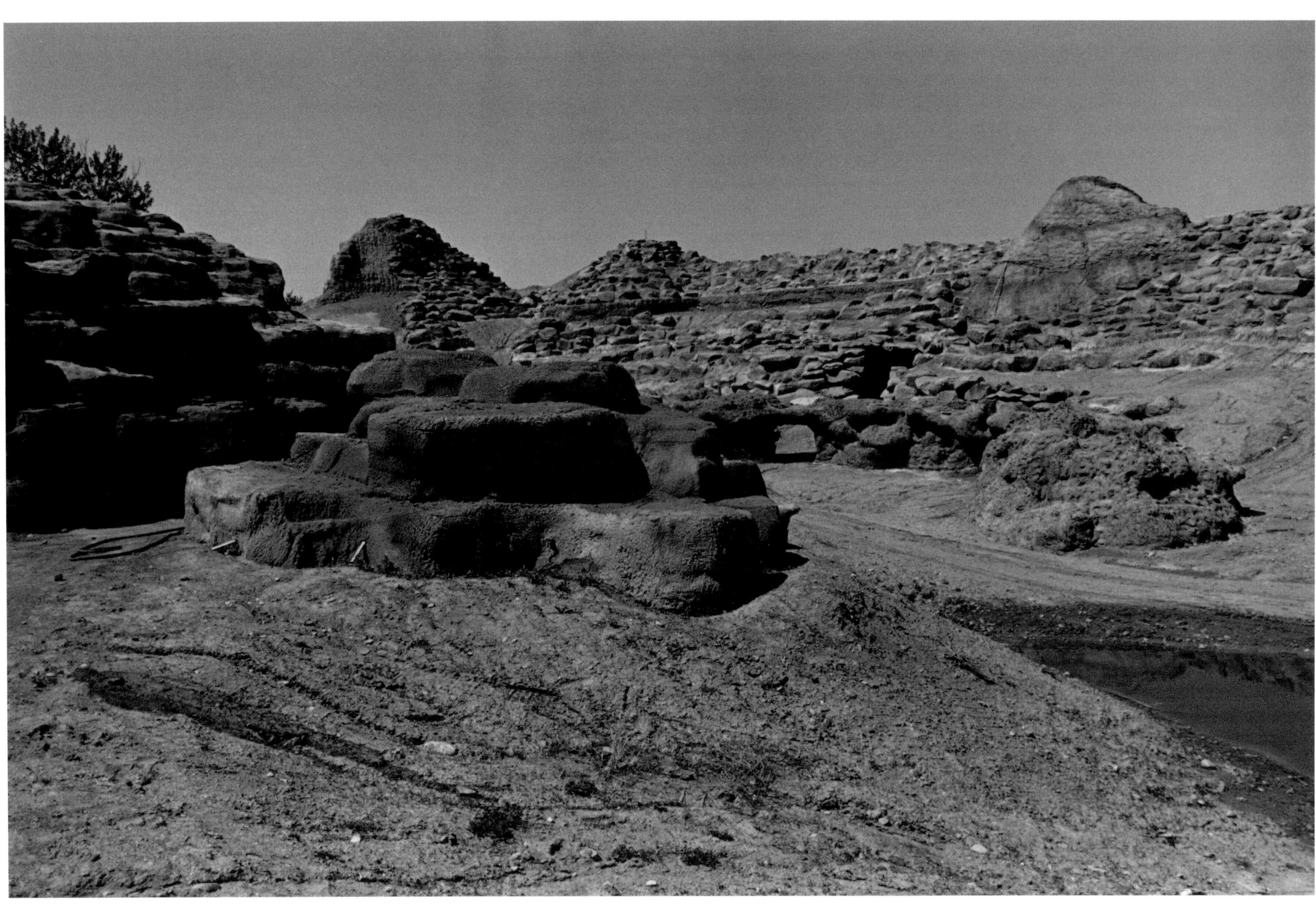

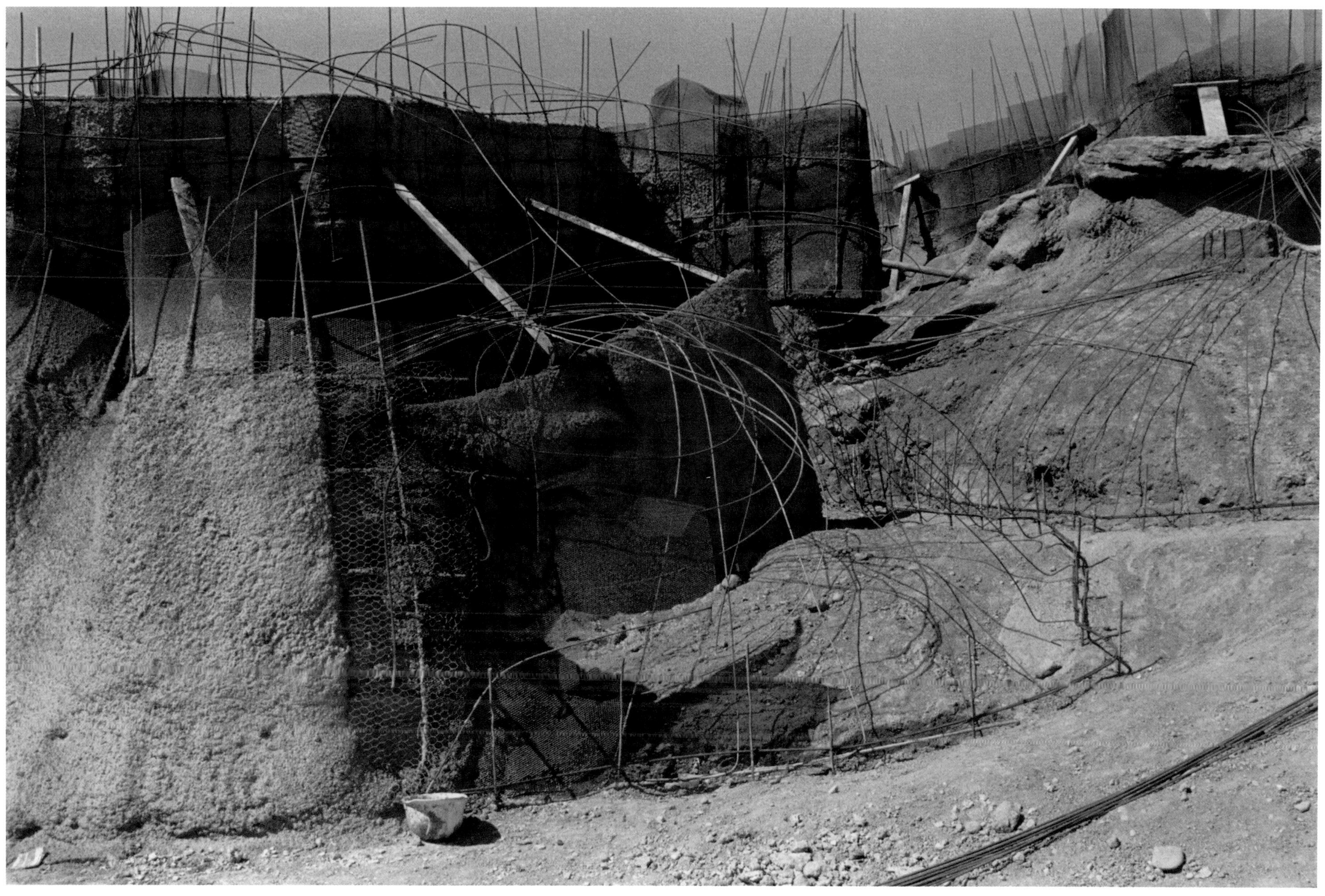

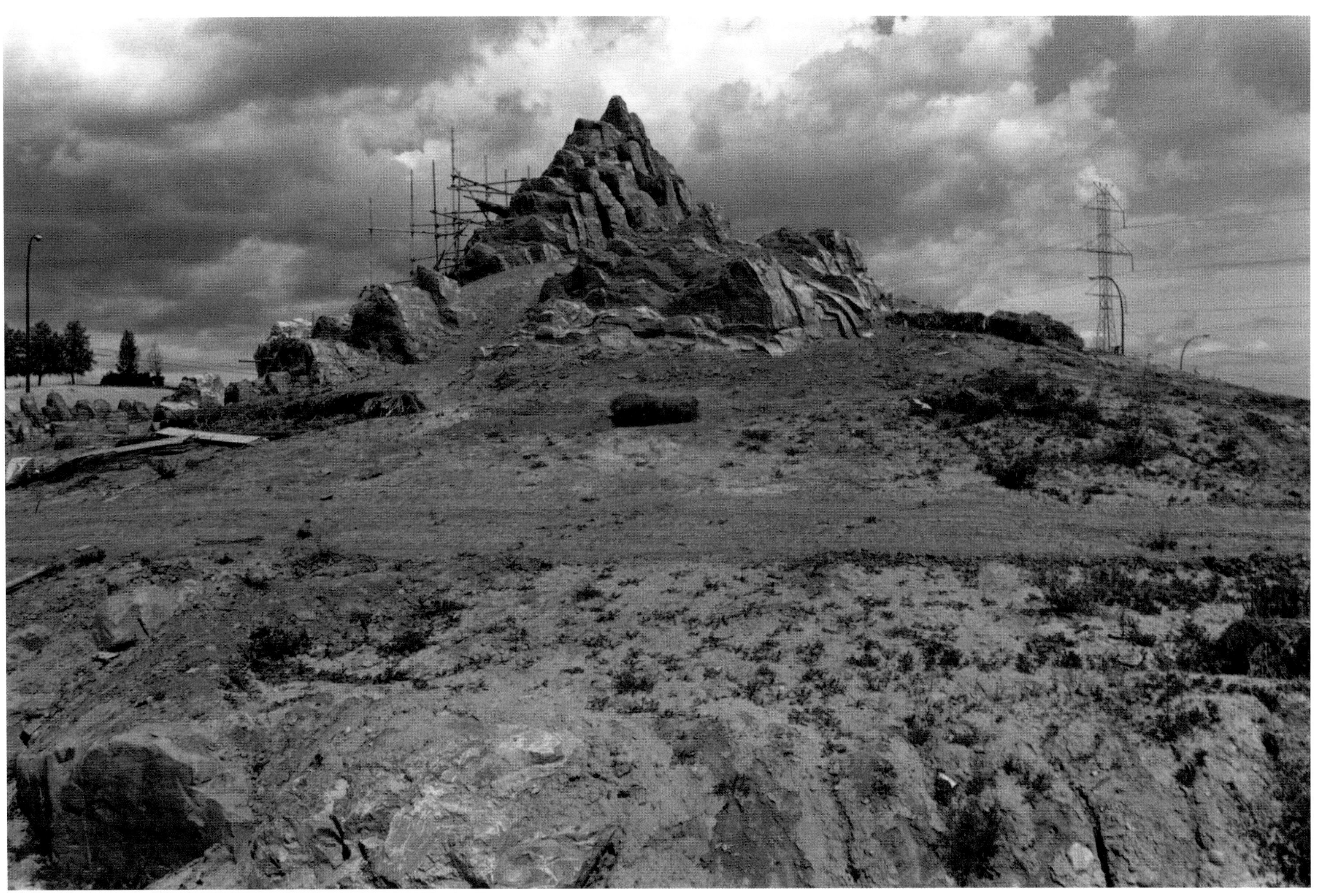

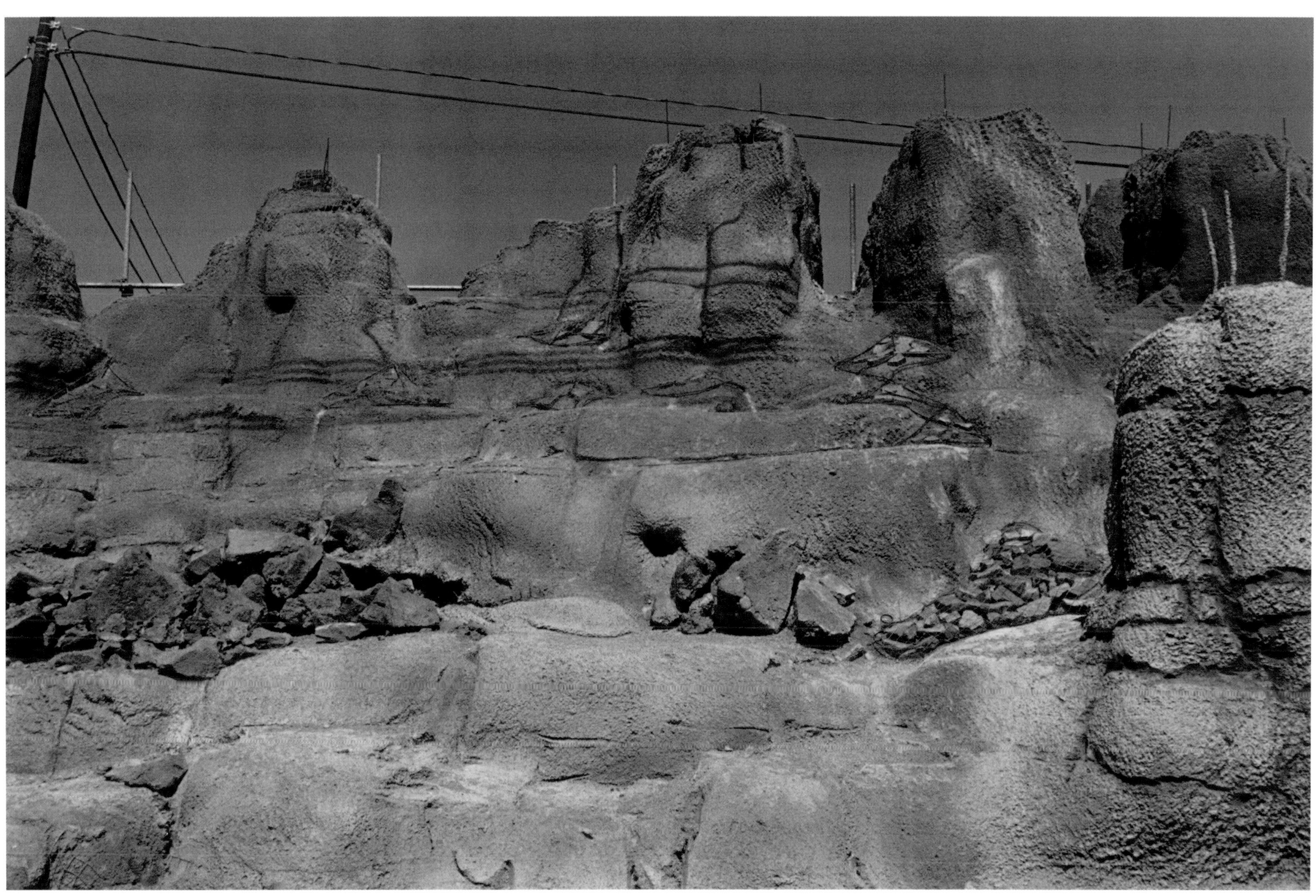

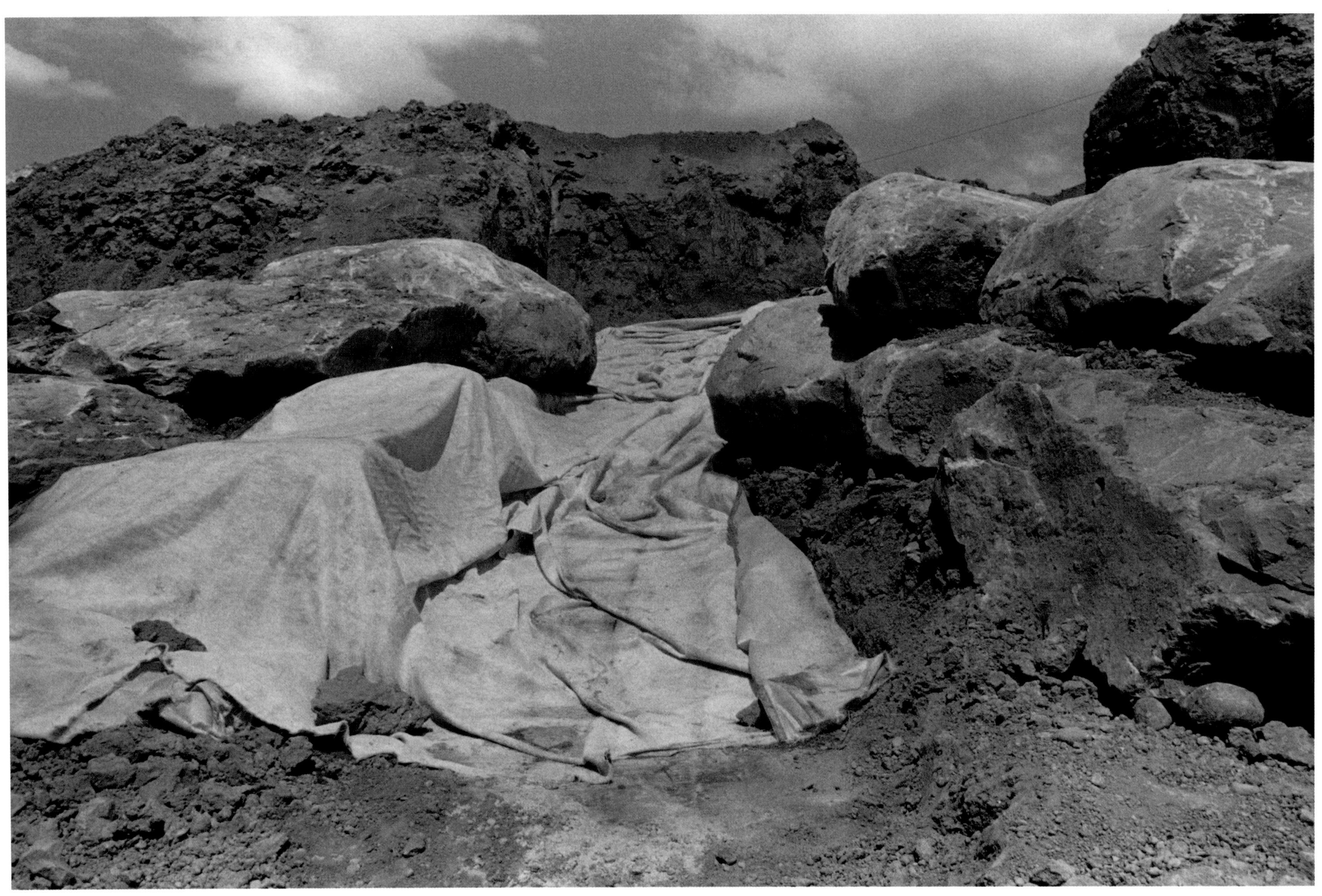

Plates 39 to 51
Calgary, Alberta
2018

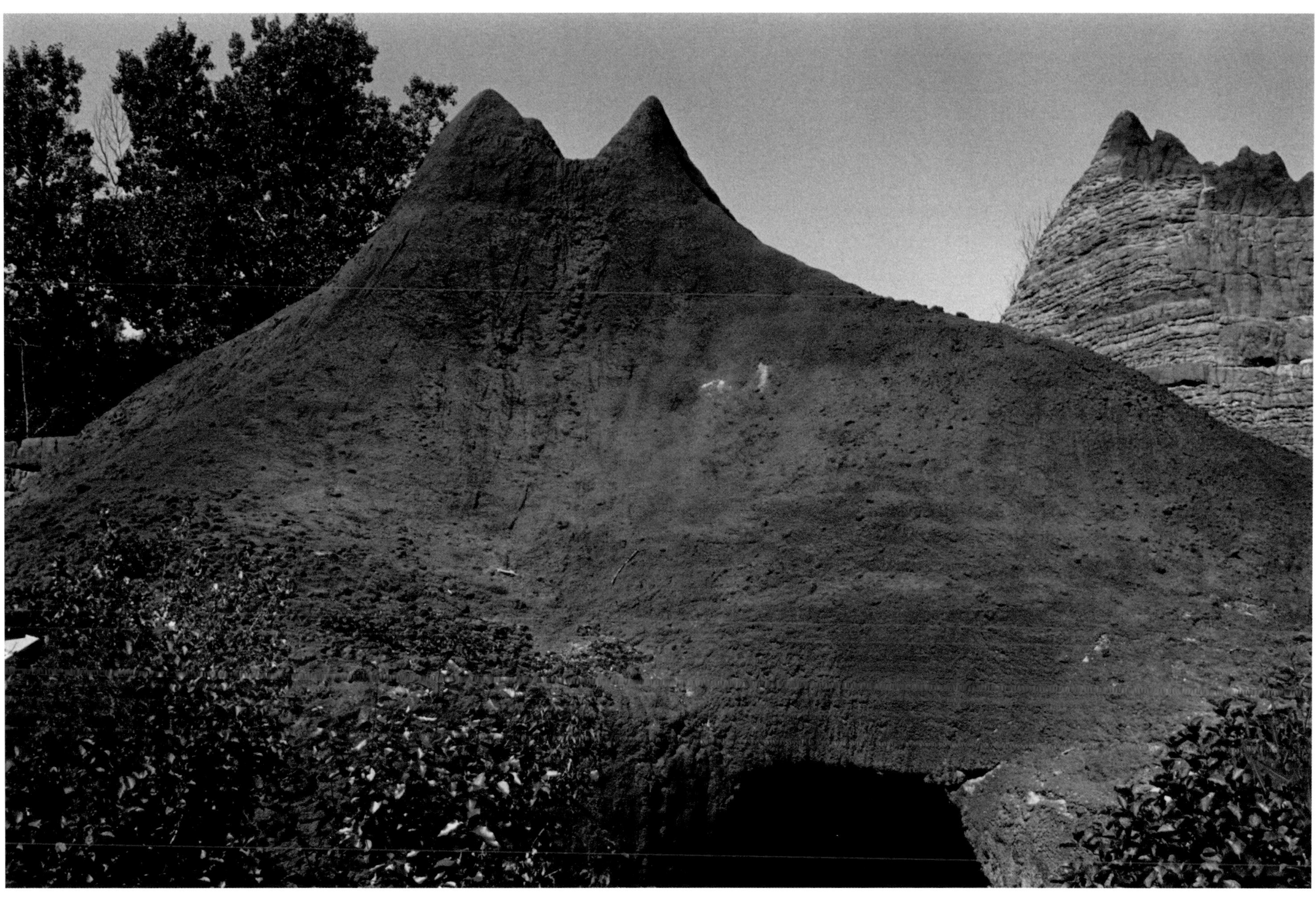

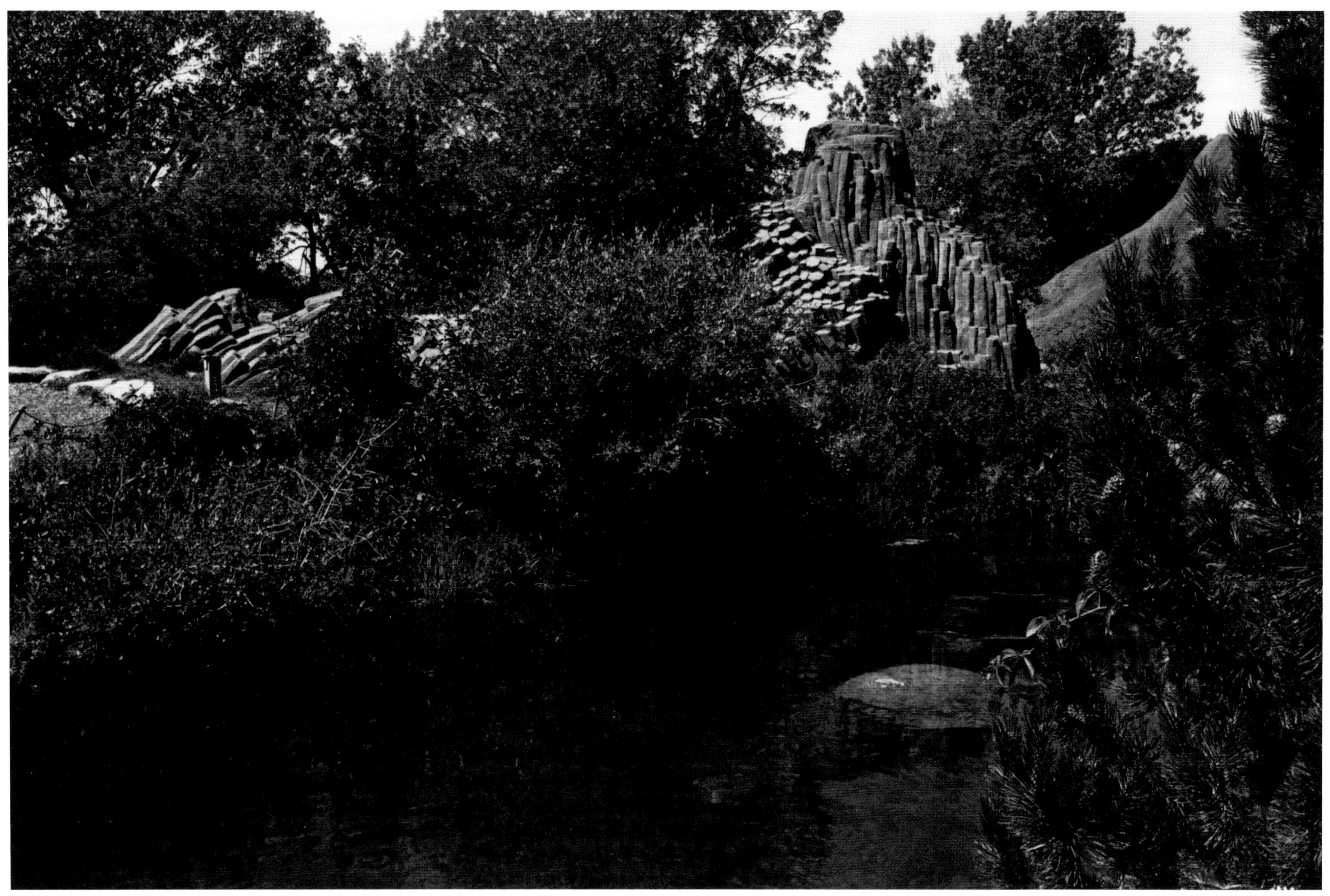

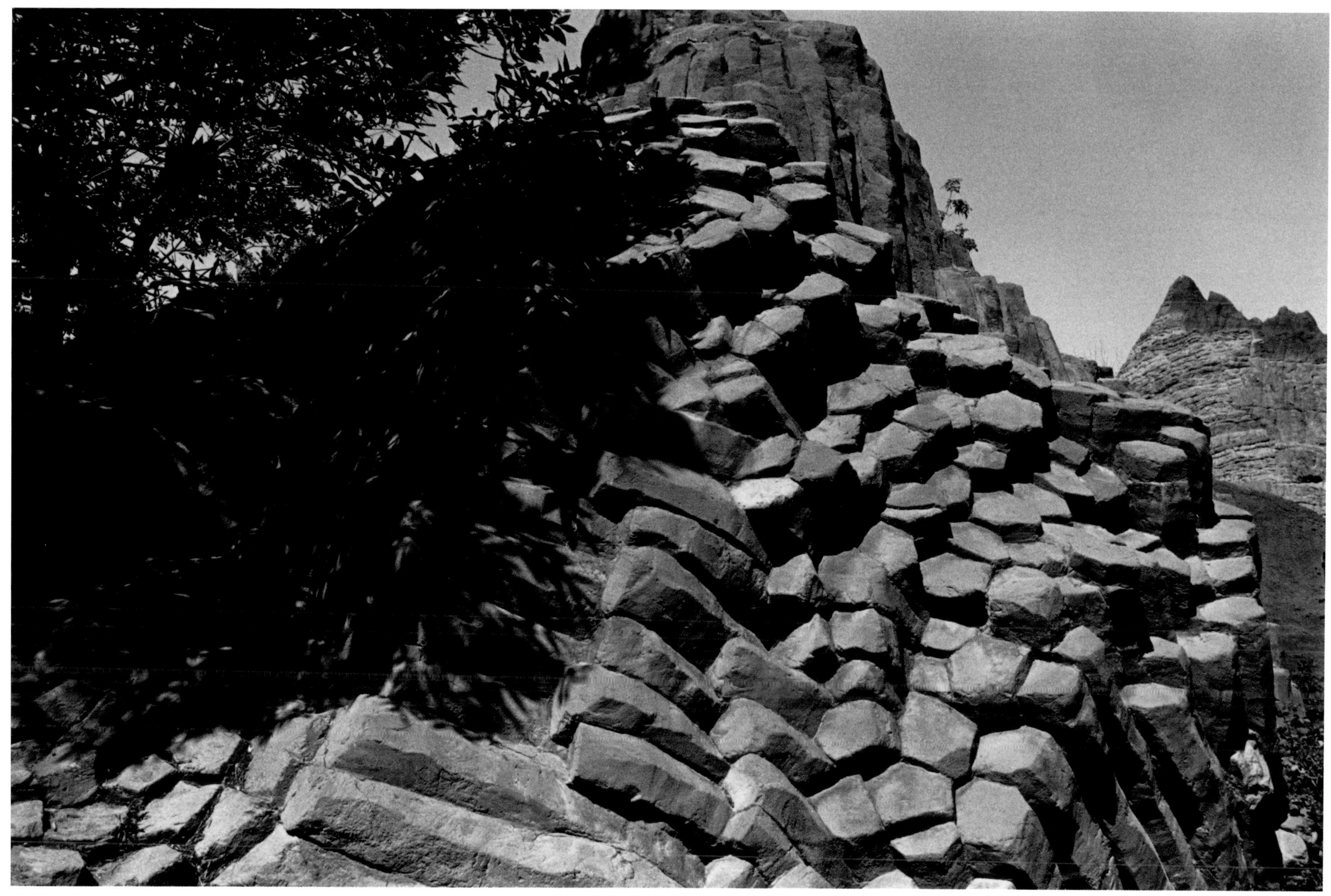

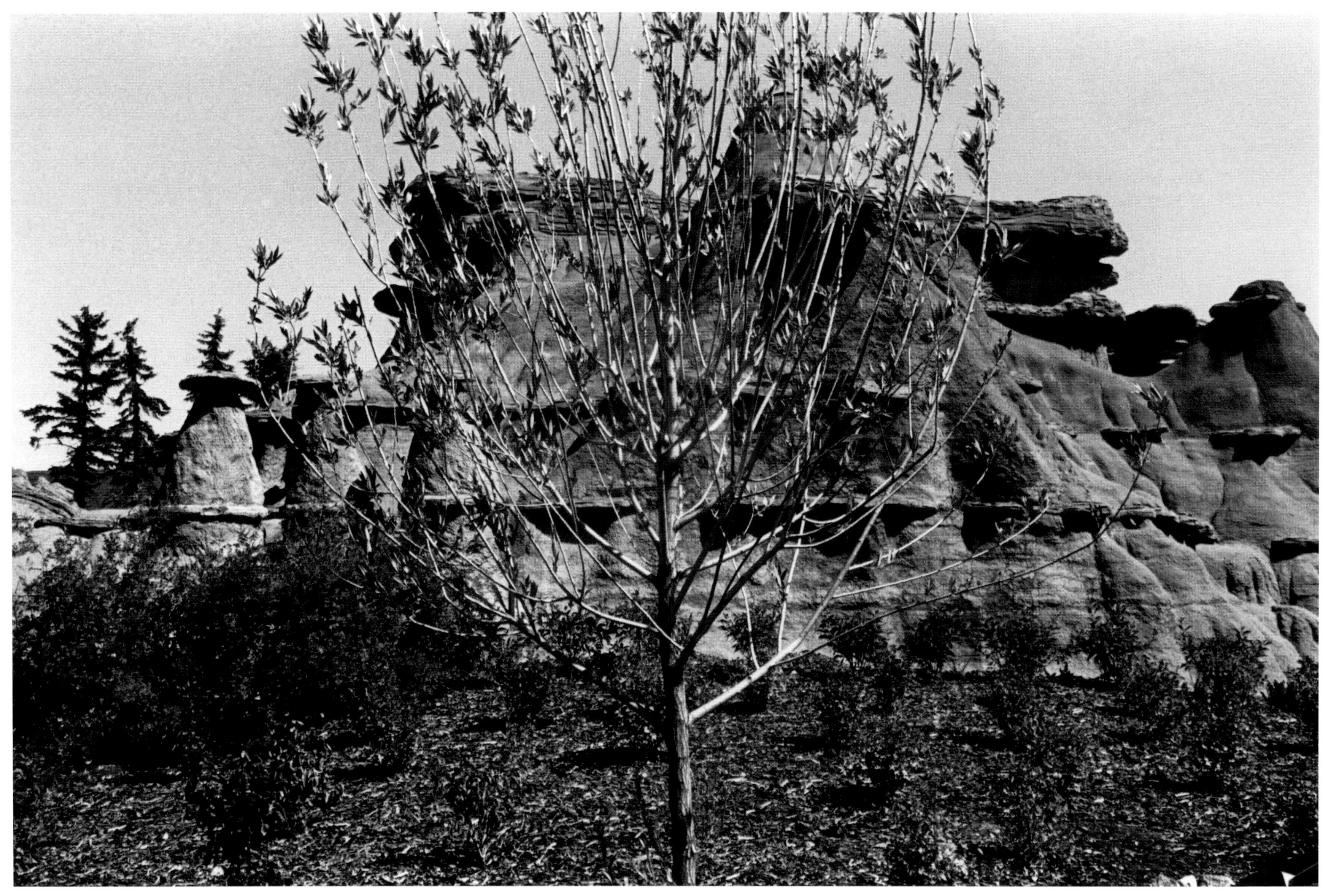

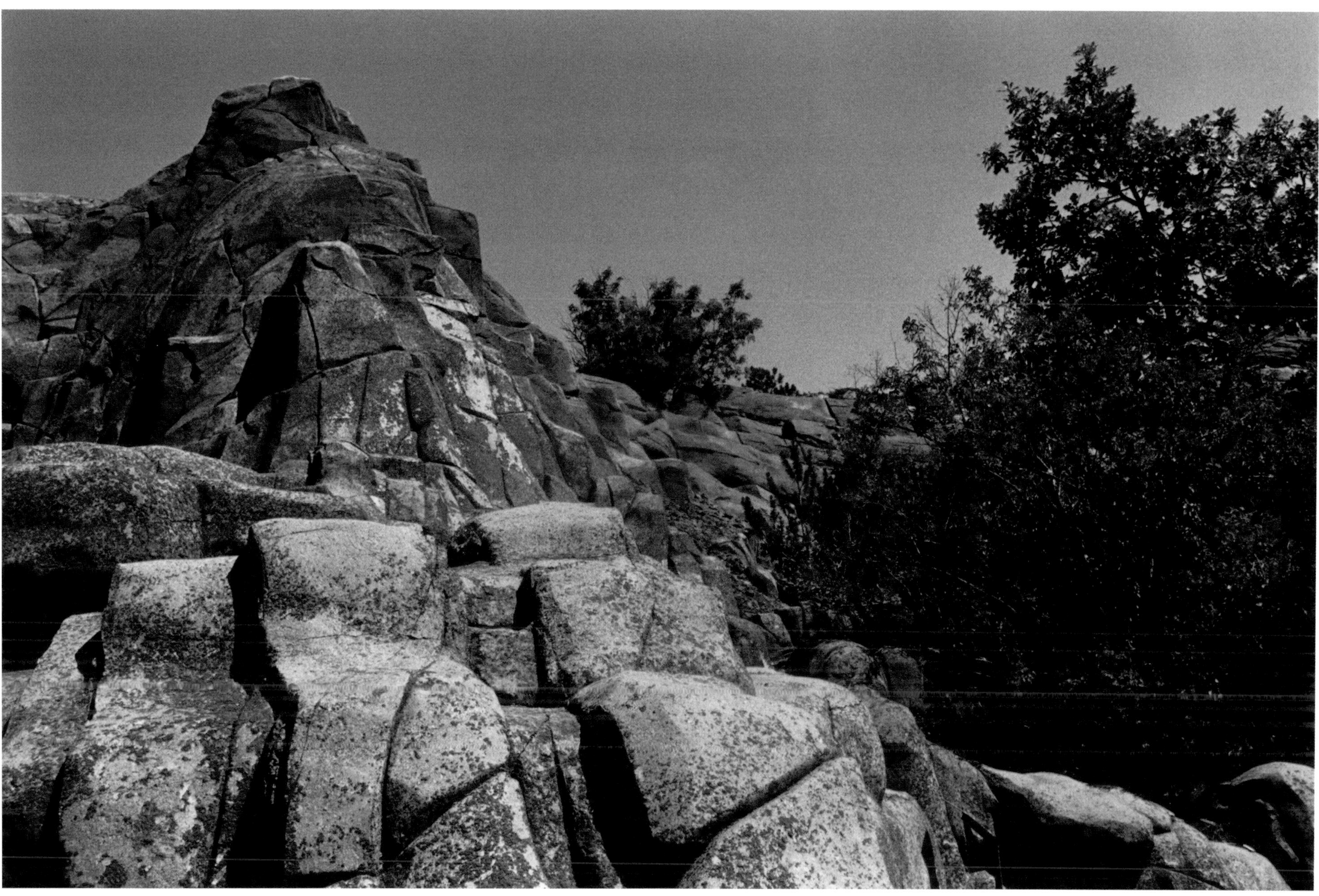

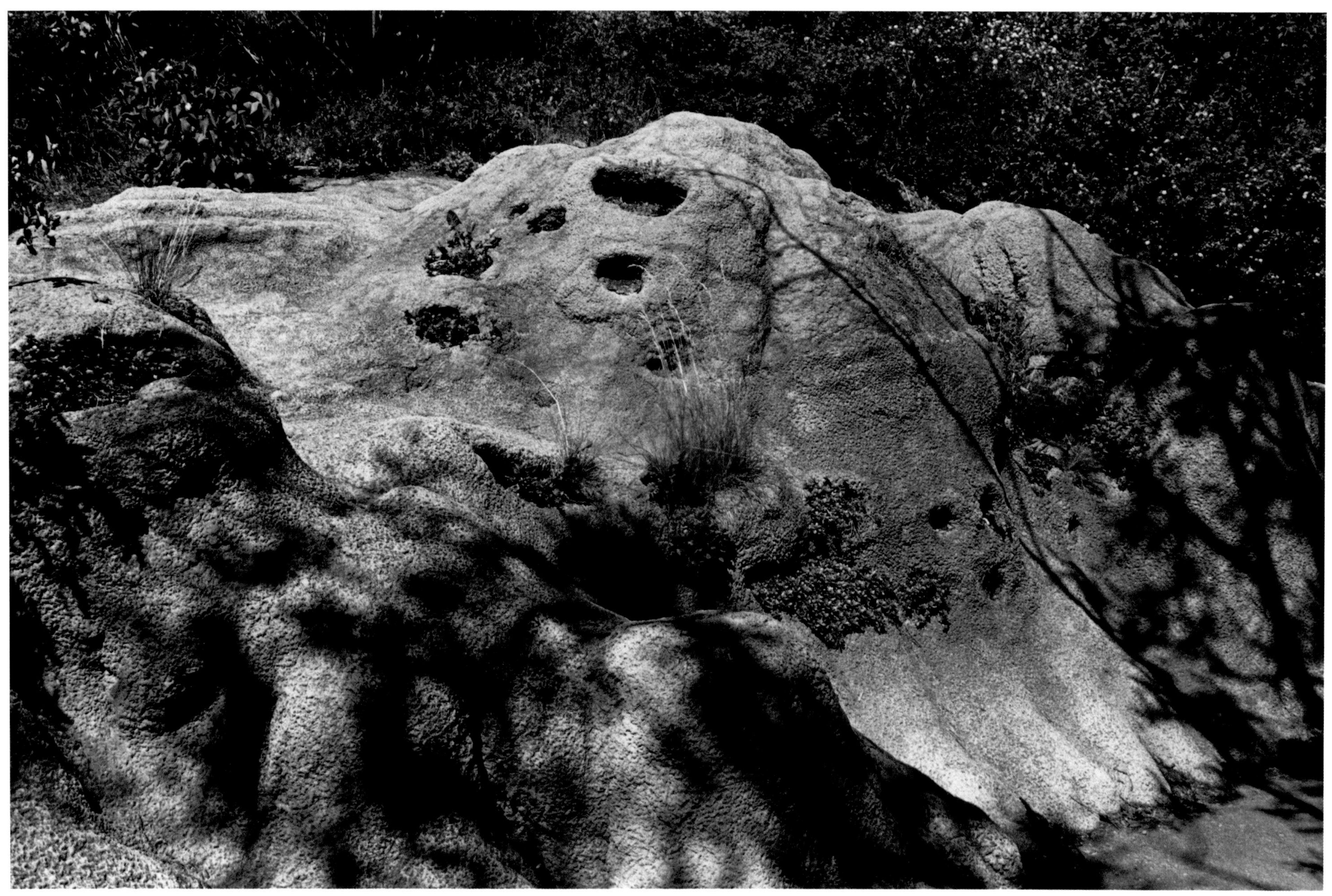

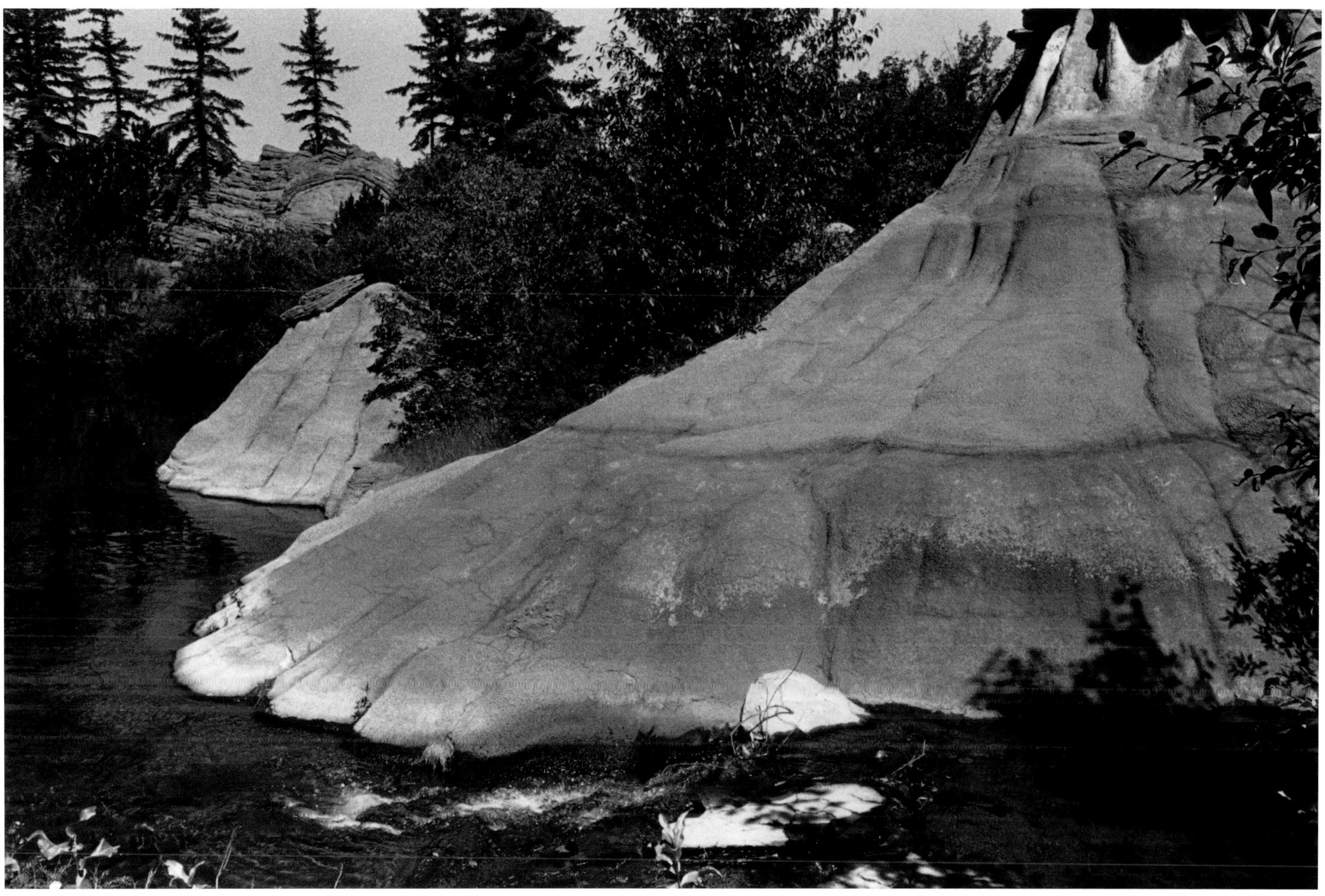

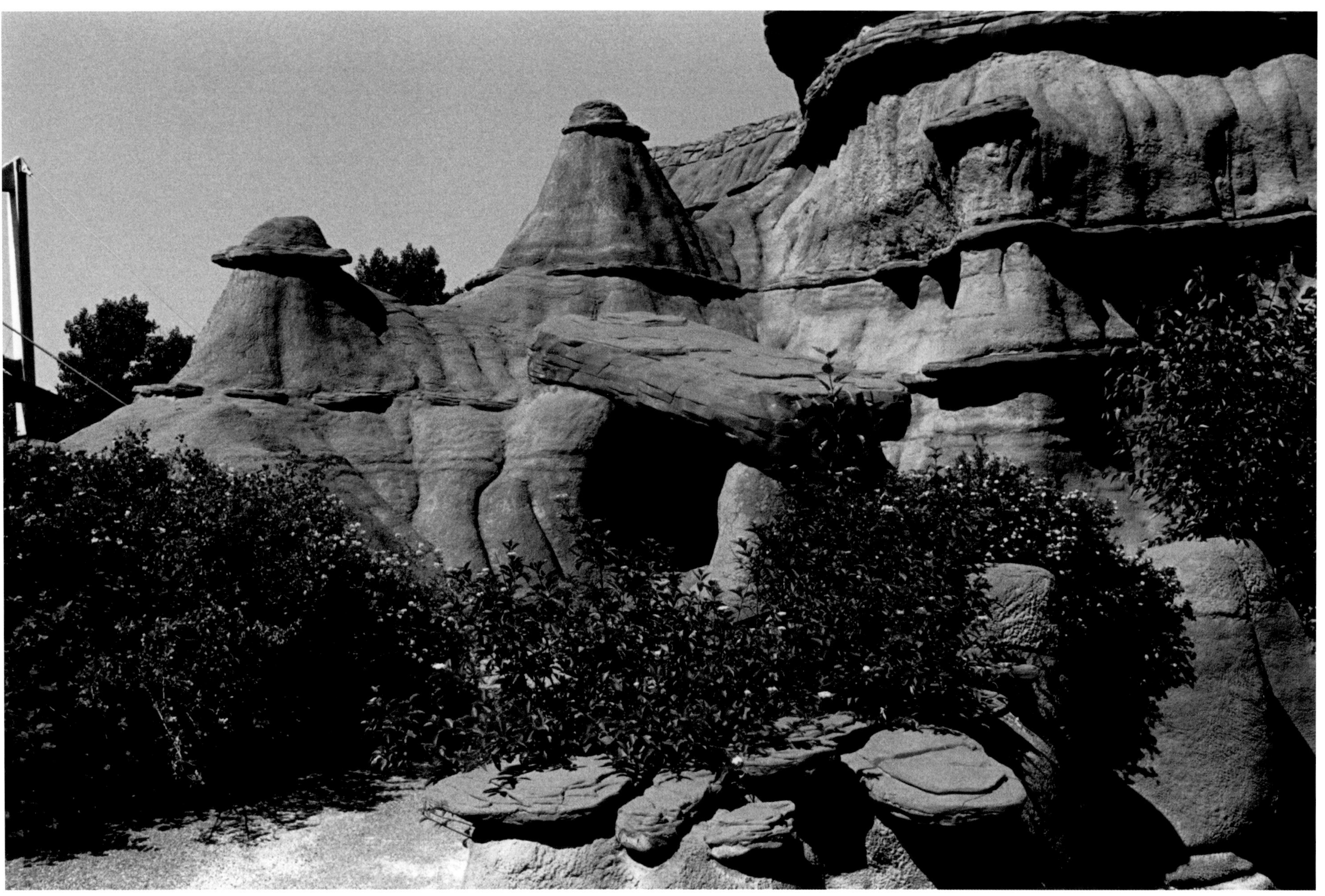

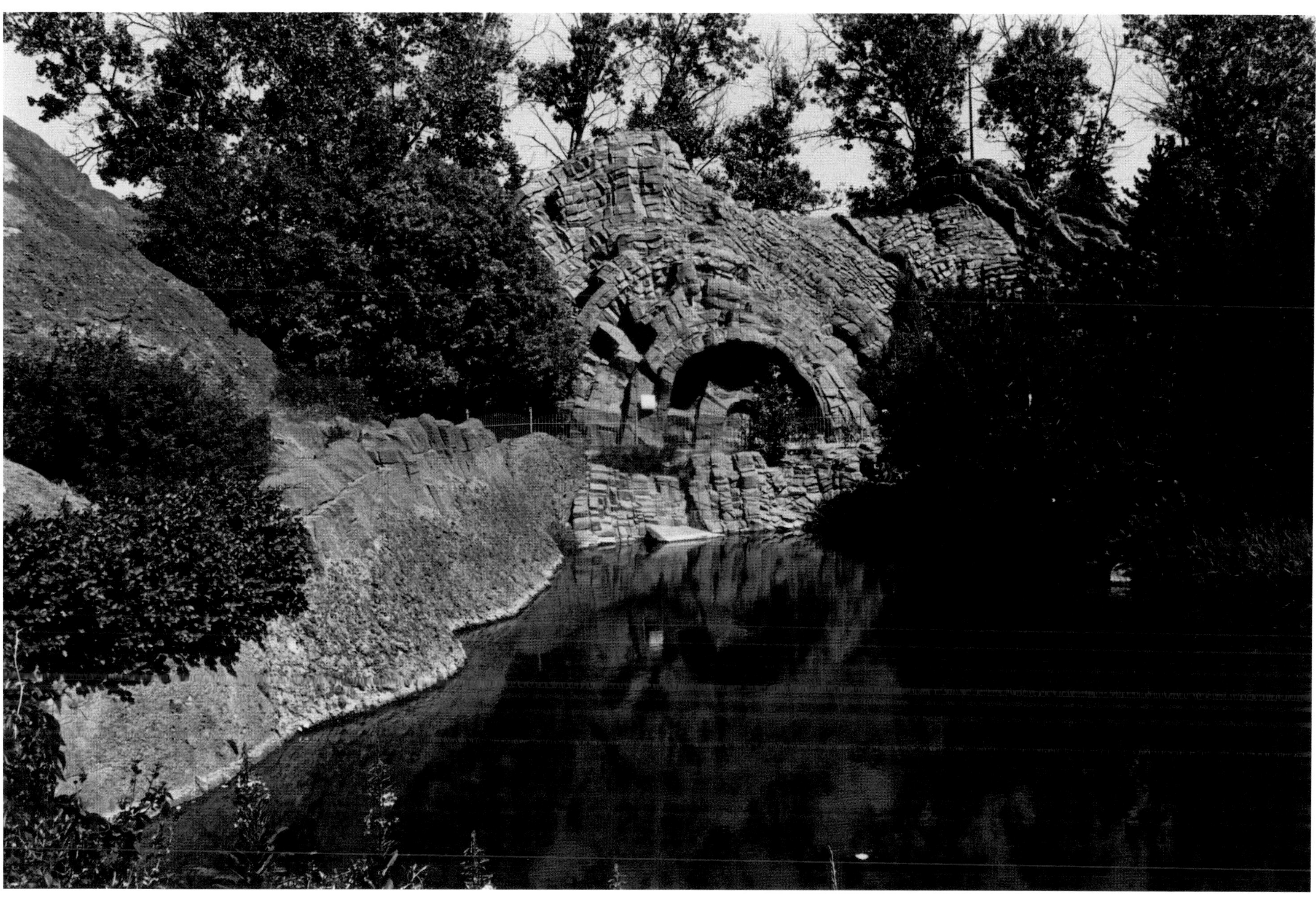

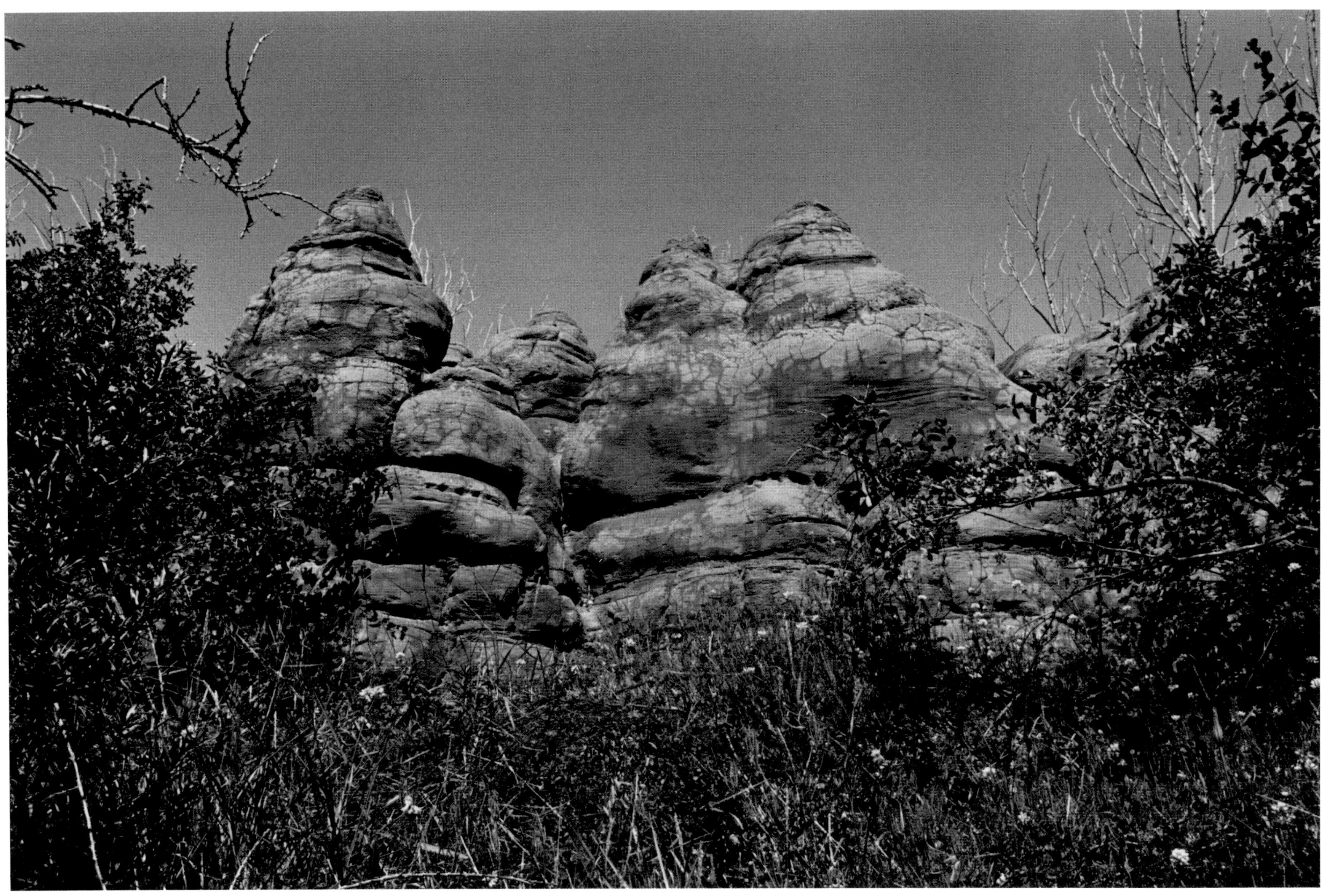

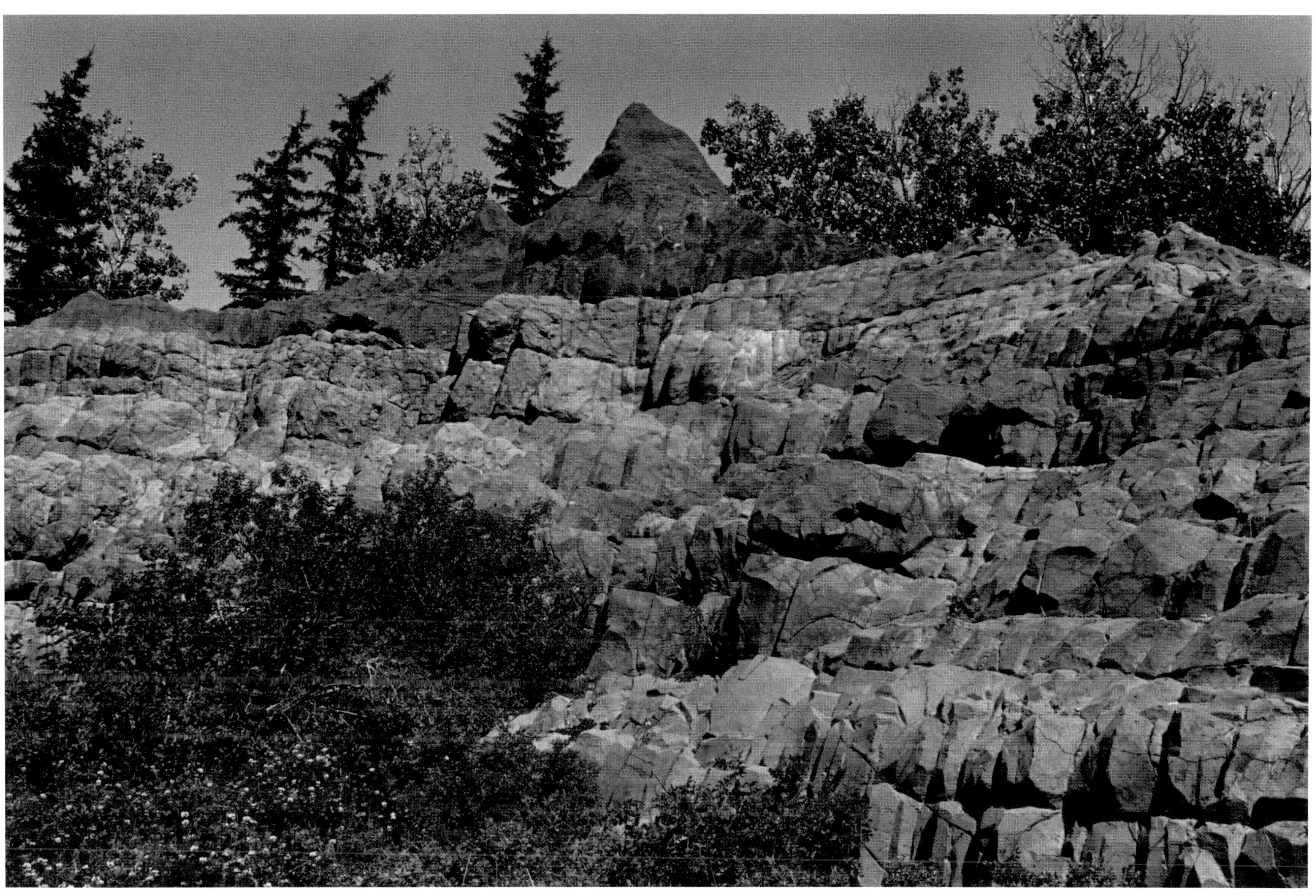

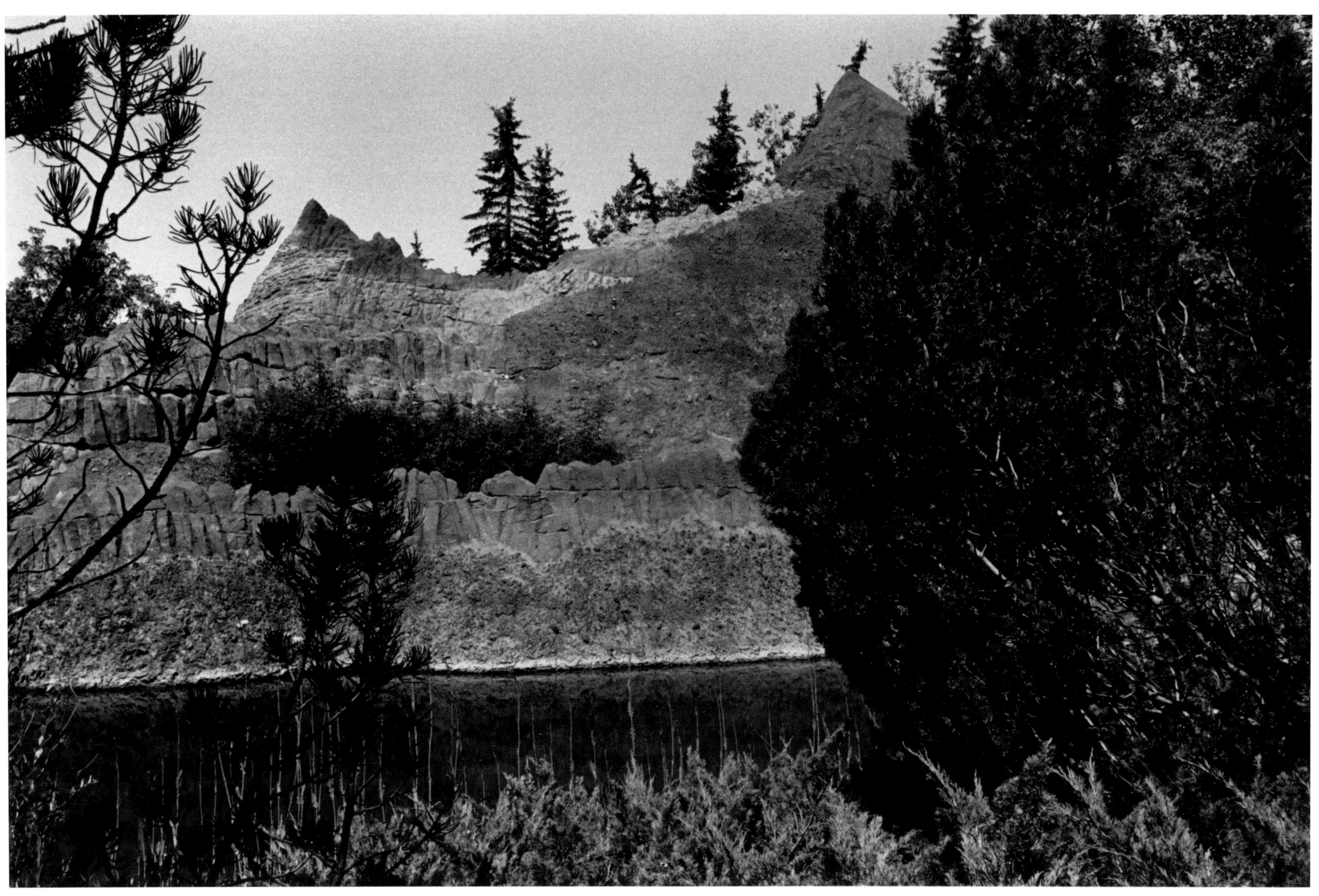

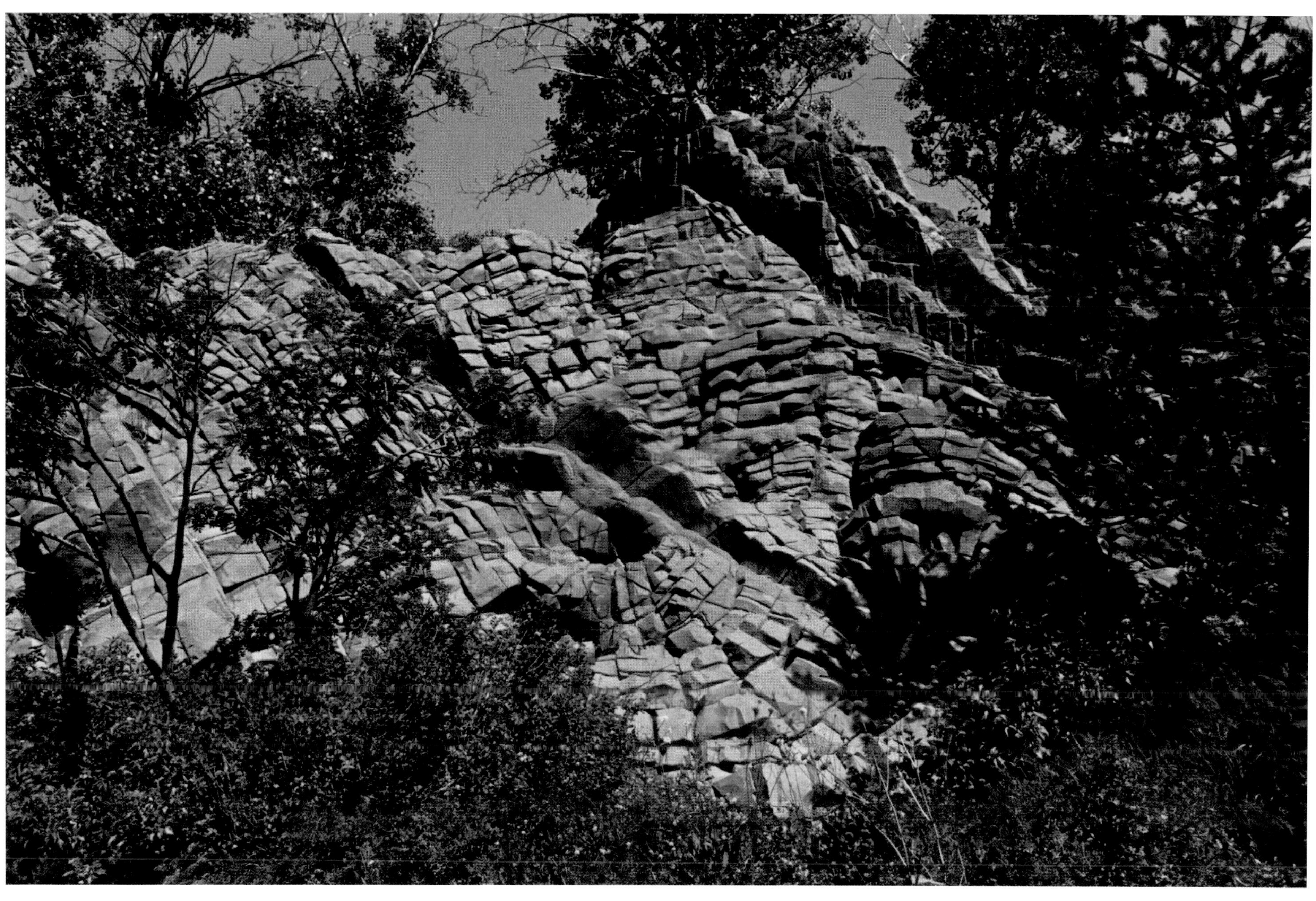

LIST OF PLATES

Silver-gelatin prints

Plates 1 to 38
Calgary, Alberta
1982

Plates 39 to 51
Calgary, Alberta
2018

BIOGRAPHIES

TERRY MUNRO is a Canadian photographer who shares his time between Calgary and Vancouver. His photographs can be found in the permanent collections of the National Gallery of Canada, Canada Council Art Bank, and the Alberta Foundation of the Arts, among others. He is a graduate of the San Francisco Art Institute in California. His book of photographs of Las Vegas Blvd, *Empire of Illusion*, was published by Black Dog Publishing in 2017.

DANIELLE SIEMENS is an art historian and museum professional based in Edmonton, Alberta on Treaty 6 Territory. She has earned degrees in Art History from the University of Alberta and Carleton University and has held internships at the National Gallery of Canada and National Gallery of Art (Washington, DC). She is currently the Curator of Interpretation and Engagement at the Art Gallery of Alberta.

Black Dog Press Limited
81 Rivington Street
London EC2A 3AY
United Kingdom

+44 (0)20 8371 4047
office@blackdogonline.com
www.blackdogonline.com

———

All opinions expressed within this publication are those
of the author and not necessarily of the publisher.

Designed by Rachel Pfleger

British Library Cataloguing-in-Publication Data.
A CIP record for this book is available from the British Library.

ISBN 978-1-912165-16-2

Printed by Kopa, Lithuania

Cover
Calgary, Alberta, 1982

■□■□ black dog press